C-763   CAREER EXAMINATION SERIES

This is your
PASSBOOK for...

Steam Fitter

Test Preparation Study Guide
Questions & Answers

COPYRIGHT NOTICE

This book is SOLELY intended for, is sold ONLY to, and its use is RESTRICTED to individual, bona fide applicants or candidates who qualify by virtue of having seriously filed applications for appropriate license, certificate, professional and/or promotional advancement, higher school matriculation, scholarship, or other legitimate requirements of education and/or governmental authorities.

This book is NOT intended for use, class instruction, tutoring, training, duplication, copying, reprinting, excerption, or adaptation, etc., by:

1) Other publishers
2) Proprietors and/or Instructors of "Coaching" and/or Preparatory Courses
3) Personnel and/or Training Divisions of commercial, industrial, and governmental organizations
4) Schools, colleges, or universities and/or their departments and staffs, including teachers and other personnel
5) Testing Agencies or Bureaus
6) Study groups which seek by the purchase of a single volume to copy and/or duplicate and/or adapt this material for use by the group as a whole without having purchased individual volumes for each of the members of the group
7) Et al.

Such persons would be in violation of appropriate Federal and State statutes.

PROVISION OF LICENSING AGREEMENTS – Recognized educational, commercial, industrial, and governmental institutions and organizations, and others legitimately engaged in educational pursuits, including training, testing, and measurement activities, may address request for a licensing agreement to the copyright owners, who will determine whether, and under what conditions, including fees and charges, the materials in this book may be used them. In other words, a licensing facility exists for the legitimate use of the material in this book on other than an individual basis. However, it is asseverated and affirmed here that the material in this book CANNOT be used without the receipt of the express permission of such a licensing agreement from the Publishers. Inquiries re licensing should be addressed to the company, attention rights and permissions department.

All rights reserved, including the right of reproduction in whole or in part, in any form or by any means, electronic or mechanical, including photocopying, recording, or by any information storage and retrieval system, without permission in writing from the Publisher.

Copyright © 2024 by
National Learning Corporation

212 Michael Drive, Syosset, NY 11791
(516) 921-8888 • www.passbooks.com
E-mail: info@passbooks.com

PUBLISHED IN THE UNITED STATES OF AMERICA

PASSBOOK® SERIES

THE *PASSBOOK® SERIES* has been created to prepare applicants and candidates for the ultimate academic battlefield – the examination room.

At some time in our lives, each and every one of us may be required to take an examination – for validation, matriculation, admission, qualification, registration, certification, or licensure.

Based on the assumption that every applicant or candidate has met the basic formal educational standards, has taken the required number of courses, and read the necessary texts, the *PASSBOOK® SERIES* furnishes the one special preparation which may assure passing with confidence, instead of failing with insecurity. Examination questions – together with answers – are furnished as the basic vehicle for study so that the mysteries of the examination and its compounding difficulties may be eliminated or diminished by a sure method.

This book is meant to help you pass your examination provided that you qualify and are serious in your objective.

The entire field is reviewed through the huge store of content information which is succinctly presented through a provocative and challenging approach – the question-and-answer method.

A climate of success is established by furnishing the correct answers at the end of each test.

You soon learn to recognize types of questions, forms of questions, and patterns of questioning. You may even begin to anticipate expected outcomes.

You perceive that many questions are repeated or adapted so that you can gain acute insights, which may enable you to score many sure points.

You learn how to confront new questions, or types of questions, and to attack them confidently and work out the correct answers.

You note objectives and emphases, and recognize pitfalls and dangers, so that you may make positive educational adjustments.

Moreover, you are kept fully informed in relation to new concepts, methods, practices, and directions in the field.

You discover that you are actually taking the examination all the time: you are preparing for the examination by "taking" an examination, not by reading extraneous and/or supererogatory textbooks.

In short, this PASSBOOK®, used directedly, should be an important factor in helping you to pass your test.

STEAM FITTER

DUTIES:
Steam Fitters, under supervision, perform work relating to installing, maintaining and repairing piping, controls and equipment for heating systems, compressed air systems, refrigerating systems, air conditioning systems, steam and hot water systems, fire suppression systems, cooling systems and sprinkler systems. They install boilers, feedwater, vacuum and condensate equipment, fuel oil piping and related auxiliary equipment; layout work from plans, specifications and sketches, and may work with welding and brazing equipment. They supervise the work of Steam Fitter's Helpers and perform related work.

SCOPE OF THE EXAMINATION
The written test may include questions on knowledge of basic principles of heating systems, air conditioning systems, refrigerating systems, compressed air systems, sprinkler systems, cooling systems, rigging, welding, soldering, and hoisting; knowledge of the specifications for pipes, hoses, fittings and other connecting fixtures; arithmetic; ability to install and repair pipe lines, hose lines, pumps, steam traps, valves, strainers and other related equipment; knowledge of the operation and maintenance of power and hand tools; scaffolding and ladders; safety; ability to interpret written instructions, blueprints, diagrams and manuals and other related areas.

HOW TO TAKE A TEST

I. YOU MUST PASS AN EXAMINATION

A. *WHAT EVERY CANDIDATE SHOULD KNOW*

Examination applicants often ask us for help in preparing for the written test. What can I study in advance? What kinds of questions will be asked? How will the test be given? How will the papers be graded?

As an applicant for a civil service examination, you may be wondering about some of these things. Our purpose here is to suggest effective methods of advance study and to describe civil service examinations.

Your chances for success on this examination can be increased if you know how to prepare. Those "pre-examination jitters" can be reduced if you know what to expect. You can even experience an adventure in good citizenship if you know why civil service exams are given.

B. *WHY ARE CIVIL SERVICE EXAMINATIONS GIVEN?*

Civil service examinations are important to you in two ways. As a citizen, you want public jobs filled by employees who know how to do their work. As a job seeker, you want a fair chance to compete for that job on an equal footing with other candidates. The best-known means of accomplishing this two-fold goal is the competitive examination.

Exams are widely publicized throughout the nation. They may be administered for jobs in federal, state, city, municipal, town or village governments or agencies.

Any citizen may apply, with some limitations, such as the age or residence of applicants. Your experience and education may be reviewed to see whether you meet the requirements for the particular examination. When these requirements exist, they are reasonable and applied consistently to all applicants. Thus, a competitive examination may cause you some uneasiness now, but it is your privilege and safeguard.

C. *HOW ARE CIVIL SERVICE EXAMS DEVELOPED?*

Examinations are carefully written by trained technicians who are specialists in the field known as "psychological measurement," in consultation with recognized authorities in the field of work that the test will cover. These experts recommend the subject matter areas or skills to be tested; only those knowledges or skills important to your success on the job are included. The most reliable books and source materials available are used as references. Together, the experts and technicians judge the difficulty level of the questions.

Test technicians know how to phrase questions so that the problem is clearly stated. Their ethics do not permit "trick" or "catch" questions. Questions may have been tried out on sample groups, or subjected to statistical analysis, to determine their usefulness.

Written tests are often used in combination with performance tests, ratings of training and experience, and oral interviews. All of these measures combine to form the best-known means of finding the right person for the right job.

II. HOW TO PASS THE WRITTEN TEST

A. NATURE OF THE EXAMINATION

To prepare intelligently for civil service examinations, you should know how they differ from school examinations you have taken. In school you were assigned certain definite pages to read or subjects to cover. The examination questions were quite detailed and usually emphasized memory. Civil service exams, on the other hand, try to discover your present ability to perform the duties of a position, plus your potentiality to learn these duties. In other words, a civil service exam attempts to predict how successful you will be. Questions cover such a broad area that they cannot be as minute and detailed as school exam questions.

In the public service similar kinds of work, or positions, are grouped together in one "class." This process is known as *position-classification*. All the positions in a class are paid according to the salary range for that class. One class title covers all of these positions, and they are all tested by the same examination.

B. FOUR BASIC STEPS

1) Study the announcement

How, then, can you know what subjects to study? Our best answer is: "Learn as much as possible about the class of positions for which you've applied." The exam will test the knowledge, skills and abilities needed to do the work.

Your most valuable source of information about the position you want is the official exam announcement. This announcement lists the training and experience qualifications. Check these standards and apply only if you come reasonably close to meeting them.

The brief description of the position in the examination announcement offers some clues to the subjects which will be tested. Think about the job itself. Review the duties in your mind. Can you perform them, or are there some in which you are rusty? Fill in the blank spots in your preparation.

Many jurisdictions preview the written test in the exam announcement by including a section called "Knowledge and Abilities Required," "Scope of the Examination," or some similar heading. Here you will find out specifically what fields will be tested.

2) Review your own background

Once you learn in general what the position is all about, and what you need to know to do the work, ask yourself which subjects you already know fairly well and which need improvement. You may wonder whether to concentrate on improving your strong areas or on building some background in your fields of weakness. When the announcement has specified "some knowledge" or "considerable knowledge," or has used adjectives like "beginning principles of..." or "advanced ... methods," you can get a clue as to the number and difficulty of questions to be asked in any given field. More questions, and hence broader coverage, would be included for those subjects which are more important in the work. Now weigh your strengths and weaknesses against the job requirements and prepare accordingly.

3) Determine the level of the position

Another way to tell how intensively you should prepare is to understand the level of the job for which you are applying. Is it the entering level? In other words, is this the position in which beginners in a field of work are hired? Or is it an intermediate or advanced level? Sometimes this is indicated by such words as "Junior" or "Senior" in the class title. Other jurisdictions use Roman numerals to designate the level – Clerk I, Clerk II, for example. The word "Supervisor" sometimes appears in the title. If the level is not indicated by the title, check the description of duties. Will you be working under very close supervision, or will you have responsibility for independent decisions in this work?

4) Choose appropriate study materials

Now that you know the subjects to be examined and the relative amount of each subject to be covered, you can choose suitable study materials. For beginning level jobs, or even advanced ones, if you have a pronounced weakness in some aspect of your training, read a modern, standard textbook in that field. Be sure it is up to date and has general coverage. Such books are normally available at your library, and the librarian will be glad to help you locate one. For entry-level positions, questions of appropriate difficulty are chosen – neither highly advanced questions, nor those too simple. Such questions require careful thought but not advanced training.

If the position for which you are applying is technical or advanced, you will read more advanced, specialized material. If you are already familiar with the basic principles of your field, elementary textbooks would waste your time. Concentrate on advanced textbooks and technical periodicals. Think through the concepts and review difficult problems in your field.

These are all general sources. You can get more ideas on your own initiative, following these leads. For example, training manuals and publications of the government agency which employs workers in your field can be useful, particularly for technical and professional positions. A letter or visit to the government department involved may result in more specific study suggestions, and certainly will provide you with a more definite idea of the exact nature of the position you are seeking.

III. KINDS OF TESTS

Tests are used for purposes other than measuring knowledge and ability to perform specified duties. For some positions, it is equally important to test ability to make adjustments to new situations or to profit from training. In others, basic mental abilities not dependent on information are essential. Questions which test these things may not appear as pertinent to the duties of the position as those which test for knowledge and information. Yet they are often highly important parts of a fair examination. For very general questions, it is almost impossible to help you direct your study efforts. What we can do is to point out some of the more common of these general abilities needed in public service positions and describe some typical questions.

1) General Information

Broad, general information has been found useful for predicting job success in some kinds of work. This is tested in a variety of ways, from vocabulary lists to questions about current events. Basic background in some field of work, such as sociology or economics, may be sampled in a group of questions. Often these are principles which have become familiar to most persons through exposure rather than through formal training. It is difficult to advise you how to study for these questions; being alert to the world around you is our best suggestion.

2) Verbal ability

An example of an ability needed in many positions is verbal or language ability. Verbal ability is, in brief, the ability to use and understand words. Vocabulary and grammar tests are typical measures of this ability. Reading comprehension or paragraph interpretation questions are common in many kinds of civil service tests. You are given a paragraph of written material and asked to find its central meaning.

3) Numerical ability

Number skills can be tested by the familiar arithmetic problem, by checking paired lists of numbers to see which are alike and which are different, or by interpreting charts and graphs. In the latter test, a graph may be printed in the test booklet which you are asked to use as the basis for answering questions.

4) Observation

A popular test for law-enforcement positions is the observation test. A picture is shown to you for several minutes, then taken away. Questions about the picture test your ability to observe both details and larger elements.

5) Following directions

In many positions in the public service, the employee must be able to carry out written instructions dependably and accurately. You may be given a chart with several columns, each column listing a variety of information. The questions require you to carry out directions involving the information given in the chart.

6) Skills and aptitudes

Performance tests effectively measure some manual skills and aptitudes. When the skill is one in which you are trained, such as typing or shorthand, you can practice. These tests are often very much like those given in business school or high school courses. For many of the other skills and aptitudes, however, no short-time preparation can be made. Skills and abilities natural to you or that you have developed throughout your lifetime are being tested.

Many of the general questions just described provide all the data needed to answer the questions and ask you to use your reasoning ability to find the answers. Your best preparation for these tests, as well as for tests of facts and ideas, is to be at your physical and mental best. You, no doubt, have your own methods of getting into an exam-taking mood and keeping "in shape." The next section lists some ideas on this subject.

IV. KINDS OF QUESTIONS

Only rarely is the "essay" question, which you answer in narrative form, used in civil service tests. Civil service tests are usually of the short-answer type. Full instructions for answering these questions will be given to you at the examination. But in case this is your first experience with short-answer questions and separate answer sheets, here is what you need to know:

1) Multiple-choice Questions

Most popular of the short-answer questions is the "multiple choice" or "best answer" question. It can be used, for example, to test for factual knowledge, ability to solve problems or judgment in meeting situations found at work.

A multiple-choice question is normally one of three types—
- It can begin with an incomplete statement followed by several possible endings. You are to find the one ending which *best* completes the statement, although some of the others may not be entirely wrong.
- It can also be a complete statement in the form of a question which is answered by choosing one of the statements listed.

- It can be in the form of a problem – again you select the best answer.

Here is an example of a multiple-choice question with a discussion which should give you some clues as to the method for choosing the right answer:

When an employee has a complaint about his assignment, the action which will *best* help him overcome his difficulty is to
  A. discuss his difficulty with his coworkers
  B. take the problem to the head of the organization
  C. take the problem to the person who gave him the assignment
  D. say nothing to anyone about his complaint

In answering this question, you should study each of the choices to find which is best. Consider choice "A" – Certainly an employee may discuss his complaint with fellow employees, but no change or improvement can result, and the complaint remains unresolved. Choice "B" is a poor choice since the head of the organization probably does not know what assignment you have been given, and taking your problem to him is known as "going over the head" of the supervisor. The supervisor, or person who made the assignment, is the person who can clarify it or correct any injustice. Choice "C" is, therefore, correct. To say nothing, as in choice "D," is unwise. Supervisors have and interest in knowing the problems employees are facing, and the employee is seeking a solution to his problem.

2) True/False Questions

The "true/false" or "right/wrong" form of question is sometimes used. Here a complete statement is given. Your job is to decide whether the statement is right or wrong.

SAMPLE: A roaming cell-phone call to a nearby city costs less than a non-roaming call to a distant city.

This statement is wrong, or false, since roaming calls are more expensive.

This is not a complete list of all possible question forms, although most of the others are variations of these common types. You will always get complete directions for answering questions. Be sure you understand *how* to mark your answers – ask questions until you do.

V. RECORDING YOUR ANSWERS

Computer terminals are used more and more today for many different kinds of exams.
For an examination with very few applicants, you may be told to record your answers in the test booklet itself. Separate answer sheets are much more common. If this separate answer sheet is to be scored by machine – and this is often the case – it is highly important that you mark your answers correctly in order to get credit.
An electronic scoring machine is often used in civil service offices because of the speed with which papers can be scored. Machine-scored answer sheets must be marked with a pencil, which will be given to you. This pencil has a high graphite content which responds to the electronic scoring machine. As a matter of fact, stray dots may register as answers, so do not let your pencil rest on the answer sheet while you are pondering the correct answer. Also, if your pencil lead breaks or is otherwise defective, ask for another.

Since the answer sheet will be dropped in a slot in the scoring machine, be careful not to bend the corners or get the paper crumpled.

The answer sheet normally has five vertical columns of numbers, with 30 numbers to a column. These numbers correspond to the question numbers in your test booklet. After each number, going across the page are four or five pairs of dotted lines. These short dotted lines have small letters or numbers above them. The first two pairs may also have a "T" or "F" above the letters. This indicates that the first two pairs only are to be used if the questions are of the true-false type. If the questions are multiple choice, disregard the "T" and "F" and pay attention only to the small letters or numbers.

Answer your questions in the manner of the sample that follows:

32. The largest city in the United States is
    A. Washington, D.C.
    B. New York City
    C. Chicago
    D. Detroit
    E. San Francisco

1) Choose the answer you think is best. (New York City is the largest, so "B" is correct.)
2) Find the row of dotted lines numbered the same as the question you are answering. (Find row number 32)
3) Find the pair of dotted lines corresponding to the answer. (Find the pair of lines under the mark "B.")
4) Make a solid black mark between the dotted lines.

VI. BEFORE THE TEST

Common sense will help you find procedures to follow to get ready for an examination. Too many of us, however, overlook these sensible measures. Indeed, nervousness and fatigue have been found to be the most serious reasons why applicants fail to do their best on civil service tests. Here is a list of reminders:

- Begin your preparation early – Don't wait until the last minute to go scurrying around for books and materials or to find out what the position is all about.
- Prepare continuously – An hour a night for a week is better than an all-night cram session. This has been definitely established. What is more, a night a week for a month will return better dividends than crowding your study into a shorter period of time.
- Locate the place of the exam – You have been sent a notice telling you when and where to report for the examination. If the location is in a different town or otherwise unfamiliar to you, it would be well to inquire the best route and learn something about the building.
- Relax the night before the test – Allow your mind to rest. Do not study at all that night. Plan some mild recreation or diversion; then go to bed early and get a good night's sleep.
- Get up early enough to make a leisurely trip to the place for the test – This way unforeseen events, traffic snarls, unfamiliar buildings, etc. will not upset you.
- Dress comfortably – A written test is not a fashion show. You will be known by number and not by name, so wear something comfortable.

- Leave excess paraphernalia at home – Shopping bags and odd bundles will get in your way. You need bring only the items mentioned in the official notice you received; usually everything you need is provided. Do not bring reference books to the exam. They will only confuse those last minutes and be taken away from you when in the test room.
- Arrive somewhat ahead of time – If because of transportation schedules you must get there very early, bring a newspaper or magazine to take your mind off yourself while waiting.
- Locate the examination room – When you have found the proper room, you will be directed to the seat or part of the room where you will sit. Sometimes you are given a sheet of instructions to read while you are waiting. Do not fill out any forms until you are told to do so; just read them and be prepared.
- Relax and prepare to listen to the instructions
- If you have any physical problem that may keep you from doing your best, be sure to tell the test administrator. If you are sick or in poor health, you really cannot do your best on the exam. You can come back and take the test some other time.

VII. AT THE TEST

The day of the test is here and you have the test booklet in your hand. The temptation to get going is very strong. Caution! There is more to success than knowing the right answers. You must know how to identify your papers and understand variations in the type of short-answer question used in this particular examination. Follow these suggestions for maximum results from your efforts:

1) Cooperate with the monitor

The test administrator has a duty to create a situation in which you can be as much at ease as possible. He will give instructions, tell you when to begin, check to see that you are marking your answer sheet correctly, and so on. He is not there to guard you, although he will see that your competitors do not take unfair advantage. He wants to help you do your best.

2) Listen to all instructions

Don't jump the gun! Wait until you understand all directions. In most civil service tests you get more time than you need to answer the questions. So don't be in a hurry. Read each word of instructions until you clearly understand the meaning. Study the examples, listen to all announcements and follow directions. Ask questions if you do not understand what to do.

3) Identify your papers

Civil service exams are usually identified by number only. You will be assigned a number; you must not put your name on your test papers. Be sure to copy your number correctly. Since more than one exam may be given, copy your exact examination title.

4) Plan your time

Unless you are told that a test is a "speed" or "rate of work" test, speed itself is usually not important. Time enough to answer all the questions will be provided, but this does not mean that you have all day. An overall time limit has been set. Divide the total time (in minutes) by the number of questions to determine the approximate time you have for each question.

5) Do not linger over difficult questions

If you come across a difficult question, mark it with a paper clip (useful to have along) and come back to it when you have been through the booklet. One caution if you do this – be sure to skip a number on your answer sheet as well. Check often to be sure that you have not lost your place and that you are marking in the row numbered the same as the question you are answering.

6) Read the questions

Be sure you know what the question asks! Many capable people are unsuccessful because they failed to *read* the questions correctly.

7) Answer all questions

Unless you have been instructed that a penalty will be deducted for incorrect answers, it is better to guess than to omit a question.

8) Speed tests

It is often better NOT to guess on speed tests. It has been found that on timed tests people are tempted to spend the last few seconds before time is called in marking answers at random – without even reading them – in the hope of picking up a few extra points. To discourage this practice, the instructions may warn you that your score will be "corrected" for guessing. That is, a penalty will be applied. The incorrect answers will be deducted from the correct ones, or some other penalty formula will be used.

9) Review your answers

If you finish before time is called, go back to the questions you guessed or omitted to give them further thought. Review other answers if you have time.

10) Return your test materials

If you are ready to leave before others have finished or time is called, take ALL your materials to the monitor and leave quietly. Never take any test material with you. The monitor can discover whose papers are not complete, and taking a test booklet may be grounds for disqualification.

VIII. EXAMINATION TECHNIQUES

1) Read the general instructions carefully. These are usually printed on the first page of the exam booklet. As a rule, these instructions refer to the timing of the examination; the fact that you should not start work until the signal and must stop work at a signal, etc. If there are any *special* instructions, such as a choice of questions to be answered, make sure that you note this instruction carefully.

2) When you are ready to start work on the examination, that is as soon as the signal has been given, read the instructions to each question booklet, underline any key words or phrases, such as *least, best, outline, describe* and the like. In this way you will tend to answer as requested rather than discover on reviewing your paper that you *listed without describing*, that you selected the *worst* choice rather than the *best* choice, etc.

3) If the examination is of the objective or multiple-choice type – that is, each question will also give a series of possible answers: A, B, C or D, and you are called upon to select the best answer and write the letter next to that answer on your answer paper – it is advisable to start answering each question in turn. There may be anywhere from 50 to 100 such questions in the three or four hours allotted and you can see how much time would be taken if you read through all the questions before beginning to answer any. Furthermore, if you come across a question or group of questions which you know would be difficult to answer, it would undoubtedly affect your handling of all the other questions.

4) If the examination is of the essay type and contains but a few questions, it is a moot point as to whether you should read all the questions before starting to answer any one. Of course, if you are given a choice – say five out of seven and the like – then it is essential to read all the questions so you can eliminate the two that are most difficult. If, however, you are asked to answer all the questions, there may be danger in trying to answer the easiest one first because you may find that you will spend too much time on it. The best technique is to answer the first question, then proceed to the second, etc.

5) Time your answers. Before the exam begins, write down the time it started, then add the time allowed for the examination and write down the time it must be completed, then divide the time available somewhat as follows:
    - If 3-1/2 hours are allowed, that would be 210 minutes. If you have 80 objective-type questions, that would be an average of 2-1/2 minutes per question. Allow yourself no more than 2 minutes per question, or a total of 160 minutes, which will permit about 50 minutes to review.
    - If for the time allotment of 210 minutes there are 7 essay questions to answer, that would average about 30 minutes a question. Give yourself only 25 minutes per question so that you have about 35 minutes to review.

6) The most important instruction is to *read each question* and make sure you know what is wanted. The second most important instruction is to *time yourself properly* so that you answer every question. The third most important instruction is to *answer every question*. Guess if you have to but include something for each question. Remember that you will receive no credit for a blank and will probably receive some credit if you write something in answer to an essay question. If you guess a letter – say "B" for a multiple-choice question – you may have guessed right. If you leave a blank as an answer to a multiple choice question, the examiners may respect your feelings but it will not add a point to your score. Some exams may penalize you for wrong answers, so in such cases *only*, you may not want to guess unless you have some basis for your answer.

7) Suggestions
    a. Objective-type questions
        1. Examine the question booklet for proper sequence of pages and questions
        2. Read all instructions carefully
        3. Skip any question which seems too difficult; return to it after all other questions have been answered
        4. Apportion your time properly; do not spend too much time on any single question or group of questions

5. Note and underline key words – *all, most, fewest, least, best, worst, same, opposite,* etc.
6. Pay particular attention to negatives
7. Note unusual option, e.g., unduly long, short, complex, different or similar in content to the body of the question
8. Observe the use of "hedging" words – *probably, may, most likely,* etc.
9. Make sure that your answer is put next to the same number as the question
10. Do not second-guess unless you have good reason to believe the second answer is definitely more correct
11. Cross out original answer if you decide another answer is more accurate; do not erase until you are ready to hand your paper in
12. Answer all questions; guess unless instructed otherwise
13. Leave time for review

b. Essay questions
1. Read each question carefully
2. Determine exactly what is wanted. Underline key words or phrases.
3. Decide on outline or paragraph answer
4. Include many different points and elements unless asked to develop any one or two points or elements
5. Show impartiality by giving pros and cons unless directed to select one side only
6. Make and write down any assumptions you find necessary to answer the questions
7. Watch your English, grammar, punctuation and choice of words
8. Time your answers; don't crowd material

8) Answering the essay question

Most essay questions can be answered by framing the specific response around several key words or ideas. Here are a few such key words or ideas:

M's: manpower, materials, methods, money, management
P's: purpose, program, policy, plan, procedure, practice, problems, pitfalls, personnel, public relations

  a. Six basic steps in handling problems:
   1. Preliminary plan and background development
   2. Collect information, data and facts
   3. Analyze and interpret information, data and facts
   4. Analyze and develop solutions as well as make recommendations
   5. Prepare report and sell recommendations
   6. Install recommendations and follow up effectiveness

  b. Pitfalls to avoid
   1. *Taking things for granted* – A statement of the situation does not necessarily imply that each of the elements is necessarily true; for example, a complaint may be invalid and biased so that all that can be taken for granted is that a complaint has been registered

2. *Considering only one side of a situation* – Wherever possible, indicate several alternatives and then point out the reasons you selected the best one
3. *Failing to indicate follow up* – Whenever your answer indicates action on your part, make certain that you will take proper follow-up action to see how successful your recommendations, procedures or actions turn out to be
4. *Taking too long in answering any single question* – Remember to time your answers properly

IX. AFTER THE TEST

Scoring procedures differ in detail among civil service jurisdictions although the general principles are the same. Whether the papers are hand-scored or graded by machine we have described, they are nearly always graded by number. That is, the person who marks the paper knows only the number – never the name – of the applicant. Not until all the papers have been graded will they be matched with names. If other tests, such as training and experience or oral interview ratings have been given, scores will be combined. Different parts of the examination usually have different weights. For example, the written test might count 60 percent of the final grade, and a rating of training and experience 40 percent. In many jurisdictions, veterans will have a certain number of points added to their grades.

After the final grade has been determined, the names are placed in grade order and an eligible list is established. There are various methods for resolving ties between those who get the same final grade – probably the most common is to place first the name of the person whose application was received first. Job offers are made from the eligible list in the order the names appear on it. You will be notified of your grade and your rank as soon as all these computations have been made. This will be done as rapidly as possible.

People who are found to meet the requirements in the announcement are called "eligibles." Their names are put on a list of eligible candidates. An eligible's chances of getting a job depend on how high he stands on this list and how fast agencies are filling jobs from the list.

When a job is to be filled from a list of eligibles, the agency asks for the names of people on the list of eligibles for that job. When the civil service commission receives this request, it sends to the agency the names of the three people highest on this list. Or, if the job to be filled has specialized requirements, the office sends the agency the names of the top three persons who meet these requirements from the general list.

The appointing officer makes a choice from among the three people whose names were sent to him. If the selected person accepts the appointment, the names of the others are put back on the list to be considered for future openings.

That is the rule in hiring from all kinds of eligible lists, whether they are for typist, carpenter, chemist, or something else. For every vacancy, the appointing officer has his choice of any one of the top three eligibles on the list. This explains why the person whose name is on top of the list sometimes does not get an appointment when some of the persons lower on the list do. If the appointing officer chooses the second or third eligible, the No. 1 eligible does not get a job at once, but stays on the list until he is appointed or the list is terminated.

X. HOW TO PASS THE INTERVIEW TEST

The examination for which you applied requires an oral interview test. You have already taken the written test and you are now being called for the interview test – the final part of the formal examination.

You may think that it is not possible to prepare for an interview test and that there are no procedures to follow during an interview. Our purpose is to point out some things you can do in advance that will help you and some good rules to follow and pitfalls to avoid while you are being interviewed.

What is an interview supposed to test?

The written examination is designed to test the technical knowledge and competence of the candidate; the oral is designed to evaluate intangible qualities, not readily measured otherwise, and to establish a list showing the relative fitness of each candidate – as measured against his competitors – for the position sought. Scoring is not on the basis of "right" and "wrong," but on a sliding scale of values ranging from "not passable" to "outstanding." As a matter of fact, it is possible to achieve a relatively low score without a single "incorrect" answer because of evident weakness in the qualities being measured.

Occasionally, an examination may consist entirely of an oral test – either an individual or a group oral. In such cases, information is sought concerning the technical knowledges and abilities of the candidate, since there has been no written examination for this purpose. More commonly, however, an oral test is used to supplement a written examination.

Who conducts interviews?

The composition of oral boards varies among different jurisdictions. In nearly all, a representative of the personnel department serves as chairman. One of the members of the board may be a representative of the department in which the candidate would work. In some cases, "outside experts" are used, and, frequently, a businessman or some other representative of the general public is asked to serve. Labor and management or other special groups may be represented. The aim is to secure the services of experts in the appropriate field.

However the board is composed, it is a good idea (and not at all improper or unethical) to ascertain in advance of the interview who the members are and what groups they represent. When you are introduced to them, you will have some idea of their backgrounds and interests, and at least you will not stutter and stammer over their names.

What should be done before the interview?

While knowledge about the board members is useful and takes some of the surprise element out of the interview, there is other preparation which is more substantive. It *is* possible to prepare for an oral interview – in several ways:

1) Keep a copy of your application and review it carefully before the interview

This may be the only document before the oral board, and the starting point of the interview. Know what education and experience you have listed there, and the sequence and dates of all of it. Sometimes the board will ask you to review the highlights of your experience for them; you should not have to hem and haw doing it.

2) Study the class specification and the examination announcement

Usually, the oral board has one or both of these to guide them. The qualities, characteristics or knowledges required by the position sought are stated in these documents. They offer valuable clues as to the nature of the oral interview. For example, if the job involves supervisory responsibilities, the announcement will usually indicate that knowledge of modern supervisory methods and the qualifications of the candidate as a supervisor will be tested. If so, you can expect such questions, frequently in the form of a hypothetical situation which you are expected to solve. NEVER go into an oral without knowledge of the duties and responsibilities of the job you seek.

3) Think through each qualification required

Try to visualize the kind of questions you would ask if you were a board member. How well could you answer them? Try especially to appraise your own knowledge and background in each area, *measured against the job sought*, and identify any areas in which you are weak. Be critical and realistic – do not flatter yourself.

4) Do some general reading in areas in which you feel you may be weak

For example, if the job involves supervision and your past experience has NOT, some general reading in supervisory methods and practices, particularly in the field of human relations, might be useful. Do NOT study agency procedures or detailed manuals. The oral board will be testing your understanding and capacity, not your memory.

5) Get a good night's sleep and watch your general health and mental attitude

You will want a clear head at the interview. Take care of a cold or any other minor ailment, and of course, no hangovers.

What should be done on the day of the interview?

Now comes the day of the interview itself. Give yourself plenty of time to get there. Plan to arrive somewhat ahead of the scheduled time, particularly if your appointment is in the fore part of the day. If a previous candidate fails to appear, the board might be ready for you a bit early. By early afternoon an oral board is almost invariably behind schedule if there are many candidates, and you may have to wait. Take along a book or magazine to read, or your application to review, but leave any extraneous material in the waiting room when you go in for your interview. In any event, relax and compose yourself.

The matter of dress is important. The board is forming impressions about you – from your experience, your manners, your attitude, and your appearance. Give your personal appearance careful attention. Dress your best, but not your flashiest. Choose conservative, appropriate clothing, and be sure it is immaculate. This is a business interview, and your appearance should indicate that you regard it as such. Besides, being well groomed and properly dressed will help boost your confidence.

Sooner or later, someone will call your name and escort you into the interview room. *This is it.* From here on you are on your own. It is too late for any more preparation. But remember, you asked for this opportunity to prove your fitness, and you are here because your request was granted.

What happens when you go in?

The usual sequence of events will be as follows: The clerk (who is often the board stenographer) will introduce you to the chairman of the oral board, who will introduce you to the other members of the board. Acknowledge the introductions before you sit down. Do not be surprised if you find a microphone facing you or a stenotypist sitting by. Oral interviews are usually recorded in the event of an appeal or other review.

Usually the chairman of the board will open the interview by reviewing the highlights of your education and work experience from your application – primarily for the benefit of the other members of the board, as well as to get the material into the record. Do not interrupt or comment unless there is an error or significant misinterpretation; if that is the case, do not hesitate. But do not quibble about insignificant matters. Also, he will usually ask you some question about your education, experience or your present job – partly to get you to start talking and to establish the interviewing "rapport." He may start the actual questioning, or turn it over to one of the other members. Frequently, each member undertakes the questioning on a particular area, one in which he is perhaps most competent, so you can expect each member to participate in the examination. Because time is limited, you may also expect some rather abrupt switches in the direction the questioning takes, so do not be upset by it. Normally, a board member will not pursue a single line of questioning unless he discovers a particular strength or weakness.

After each member has participated, the chairman will usually ask whether any member has any further questions, then will ask you if you have anything you wish to add. Unless you are expecting this question, it may floor you. Worse, it may start you off on an extended, extemporaneous speech. The board is not usually seeking more information. The question is principally to offer you a last opportunity to present further qualifications or to indicate that you have nothing to add. So, if you feel that a significant qualification or characteristic has been overlooked, it is proper to point it out in a sentence or so. Do not compliment the board on the thoroughness of their examination – they have been sketchy, and you know it. If you wish, merely say, "No thank you, I have nothing further to add." This is a point where you can "talk yourself out" of a good impression or fail to present an important bit of information. Remember, *you close the interview yourself*.

The chairman will then say, "That is all, Mr. _____, thank you." Do not be startled; the interview is over, and quicker than you think. Thank him, gather your belongings and take your leave. Save your sigh of relief for the other side of the door.

How to put your best foot forward

Throughout this entire process, you may feel that the board individually and collectively is trying to pierce your defenses, seek out your hidden weaknesses and embarrass and confuse you. Actually, this is not true. They are obliged to make an appraisal of your qualifications for the job you are seeking, and they want to see you in your best light. Remember, they must interview all candidates and a non-cooperative candidate may become a failure in spite of their best efforts to bring out his qualifications. Here are 15 suggestions that will help you:

1) Be natural – Keep your attitude confident, not cocky

If you are not confident that you can do the job, do not expect the board to be. Do not apologize for your weaknesses, try to bring out your strong points. The board is interested in a positive, not negative, presentation. Cockiness will antagonize any board member and make him wonder if you are covering up a weakness by a false show of strength.

2) Get comfortable, but don't lounge or sprawl

Sit erectly but not stiffly. A careless posture may lead the board to conclude that you are careless in other things, or at least that you are not impressed by the importance of the occasion. Either conclusion is natural, even if incorrect. Do not fuss with your clothing, a pencil or an ashtray. Your hands may occasionally be useful to emphasize a point; do not let them become a point of distraction.

3) Do not wisecrack or make small talk

This is a serious situation, and your attitude should show that you consider it as such. Further, the time of the board is limited – they do not want to waste it, and neither should you.

4) Do not exaggerate your experience or abilities

In the first place, from information in the application or other interviews and sources, the board may know more about you than you think. Secondly, you probably will not get away with it. An experienced board is rather adept at spotting such a situation, so do not take the chance.

5) If you know a board member, do not make a point of it, yet do not hide it

Certainly you are not fooling him, and probably not the other members of the board. Do not try to take advantage of your acquaintanceship – it will probably do you little good.

6) Do not dominate the interview

Let the board do that. They will give you the clues – do not assume that you have to do all the talking. Realize that the board has a number of questions to ask you, and do not try to take up all the interview time by showing off your extensive knowledge of the answer to the first one.

7) Be attentive

You only have 20 minutes or so, and you should keep your attention at its sharpest throughout. When a member is addressing a problem or question to you, give him your undivided attention. Address your reply principally to him, but do not exclude the other board members.

8) Do not interrupt

A board member may be stating a problem for you to analyze. He will ask you a question when the time comes. Let him state the problem, and wait for the question.

9) Make sure you understand the question

Do not try to answer until you are sure what the question is. If it is not clear, restate it in your own words or ask the board member to clarify it for you. However, do not haggle about minor elements.

10) Reply promptly but not hastily

A common entry on oral board rating sheets is "candidate responded readily," or "candidate hesitated in replies." Respond as promptly and quickly as you can, but do not jump to a hasty, ill-considered answer.

11) Do not be peremptory in your answers

A brief answer is proper – but do not fire your answer back. That is a losing game from your point of view. The board member can probably ask questions much faster than you can answer them.

12) Do not try to create the answer you think the board member wants

He is interested in what kind of mind you have and how it works – not in playing games. Furthermore, he can usually spot this practice and will actually grade you down on it.

13) Do not switch sides in your reply merely to agree with a board member

Frequently, a member will take a contrary position merely to draw you out and to see if you are willing and able to defend your point of view. Do not start a debate, yet do not surrender a good position. If a position is worth taking, it is worth defending.

14) Do not be afraid to admit an error in judgment if you are shown to be wrong
The board knows that you are forced to reply without any opportunity for careful consideration. Your answer may be demonstrably wrong. If so, admit it and get on with the interview.

15) Do not dwell at length on your present job
The opening question may relate to your present assignment. Answer the question but do not go into an extended discussion. You are being examined for a *new* job, not your present one. As a matter of fact, try to phrase ALL your answers in terms of the job for which you are being examined.

Basis of Rating
Probably you will forget most of these "do's" and "don'ts" when you walk into the oral interview room. Even remembering them all will not ensure you a passing grade. Perhaps you did not have the qualifications in the first place. But remembering them will help you to put your best foot forward, without treading on the toes of the board members.

Rumor and popular opinion to the contrary notwithstanding, an oral board wants you to make the best appearance possible. They know you are under pressure – but they also want to see how you respond to it as a guide to what your reaction would be under the pressures of the job you seek. They will be influenced by the degree of poise you display, the personal traits you show and the manner in which you respond.

ABOUT THIS BOOK

This book contains tests divided into Examination Sections. Go through each test, answering every question in the margin. We have also attached a sample answer sheet at the back of the book that can be removed and used. At the end of each test look at the answer key and check your answers. On the ones you got wrong, look at the right answer choice and learn. Do not fill in the answers first. Do not memorize the questions and answers, but understand the answer and principles involved. On your test, the questions will likely be different from the samples. Questions are changed and new ones added. If you understand these past questions you should have success with any changes that arise. Tests may consist of several types of questions. We have additional books on each subject should more study be advisable or necessary for you. Finally, the more you study, the better prepared you will be. This book is intended to be the last thing you study before you walk into the examination room. Prior study of relevant texts is also recommended. NLC publishes some of these in our Fundamental Series. Knowledge and good sense are important factors in passing your exam. Good luck also helps. So now study this Passbook, absorb the material contained within and take that knowledge into the examination. Then do your best to pass that exam.

EXAMINATION SECTION

EXAMINATION SECTION
TEST 1

DIRECTIONS: Each question or incomplete statement is followed by several suggested answers or completions. Select the one that BEST answers the question or completes the statement. *PRINT THE LETTER OF THE CORRECT ANSWER IN THE SPACE AT THE RIGHT.*

1. Two 6" steam lines are to be run side by side. They are to carry saturated steam at 100 lbs. per sq.in. gage pressure and are to be insulated with double standard thickness 85% magnesia covering.
If the clear space between these two lines, after being covered, is to be not less than
6", then the MINIMUM center to center distance at which these lines are to be installed should be NOT LESS than

   A. 12.5"   B. 19.0"   C. 17.5"   D. 14.5"

1.____

Questions 2-5.

DIRECTIONS: Questions 2 through 5, inclusive, are based upon the material given in the following paragraph.

Safety valves are required to operate without chattering and to be set to close after blowing down not more than 4% of the set pressure, but not less than 2 lbs. in any case. For pressure between 100 and 300 lbs., inclusive, the blow down is required to be not less than 2% of the set pressure. The blow down adjustment is made and sealed by the manufacturer. The popping-point tolerance plus or minus is required not to exceed 2 lbs. for pressure up to and including 70 lbs., 3 lbs. for pressure 71 to 300 lbs., and 10 lbs. for pressure over 300 lbs.

2. A boiler is being installed to operate at a maximum allowable pressure of 10 lbs., and the safety valve has been set to blow at this pressure. This valve should close after the boiler blows down to not more than lbs.

   A. 9.6   B. 4.0   C. 9.8   D. 8.0

2.____

3. A boiler is being installed to operate at a maximum allowable working pressure of 300 lbs., and the safety valve is set to blow at this pressure. This valve should close after the boiler blows down to not more than _____ lbs.

   A. 204   B. 298   C. 12   D. 6

3.____

4. A sealed safety valve is to be installed on a superheater header in a power steam generating plant. The marking on this valve shows that it is set to pop at 425 lbs. This valve would operate satisfactorily if it popped at either _____ lbs.

   A. 425 or 445
   C. 372.5 or 467.5
   B. 415 or 435
   D. 412.25 or 437.75

4.____

1

5. A sealed safety valve is to be installed on a boiler in a high pressure steam generating station. The marking on the valve shows that it is set to pop at 300 lbs. This valve would operate satisfactorily if it popped at either _____ lbs.

   A. 290 or 310
   B. 297 or 303
   C. 291 or 309
   D. 288 or 312

6. In a steam generating plant, the feedwater pumps are of the steam driven reciprocating duplex type. Steam at boiler pressure, 100 lbs./sq.in., is used to drive these pumps. The pumps are designed to work against a head of 150 lbs./sq.in., and the steam pistons have a diameter of 3 1/2".
   Under the above conditions, the water plungers should have a diameter, in inches, MOST NEARLY equal to

   A. 3.85"
   B. 3.26"
   C. 2.25"
   D. 2.86"

7. In a power steam generating station, an auxiliary superheated steam supply for auxiliary machinery service is taken through a header system from the main superheated steam system. The plans and specifications call for a stop-and-check to be installed in this header where it connects to the main superheated steam system.
   This is commonly done to

   A. simplify any maintenance work on auxiliary equipment
   B. do away with the need for desuperheating equipment
   C. prevent excessive pressures in the auxiliary superheated steam supply
   D. prevent back feeding or short circuits through the auxiliary superheated steam supply

8. Two five-part *block and falls* are being used to lift a length of steam pipe which weighs one-half ton. Two slings are used, one for each block and fall. The theoretical pull which each of two men would have to give, neglecting friction, in order to lift the pipe is MOST NEARLY _____ lbs.

   A. 200
   B. 100
   C. 150
   D. 175

9. Very often, in lifting pipe or auxiliaries into place, a man will mouse the hook of the lifting device after the sling has been placed in the hook. By so doing, the man

   A. increases the strength of the sling
   B. keeps the sling from leaving the hook or becoming unhooked
   C. keeps the sling from slipping through the hook
   D. increases the weight which may be lifted

10. While using some rope on a particular job, it is found necessary to tie the ends of two ropes together. It is desirable to do this in such a way that the knot won't slip. The SIMPLEST knot which one can use for this purpose is the _____ knot.

    A. square
    B. granny
    C. figure-eight
    D. clove hitch

11. A steamfitter at his work may, from time to time, use tannic acid (5% solution) for the

    A. cleaning and preparing of metal surfaces before brazing
    B. treating of minor cuts and sprains suffered on the job
    C. treatment of first and second degree burns
    D. treatment of headaches and minor stomach disorders

11.____

12. In the erection of a high pressure steam main, it becomes necessary to lift a steam manifold, which weighs 2 tons, into position. Tackle is arranged to limit the stress in any one of the parts to 800 lbs.
    The SMALLEST diameter manila rope which should be used is _____ lbs. breaking strength).

    A. 1/2" (2650)   B. 7/16" (1750)
    C. 5/8" (4400)   D. 7/8" (7700)

12.____

13. With respect to *close-link chain* hoists, it has been observed that chain wear can be reduced considerably by occasional lubrication. The life of a chain can also be prolonged by frequent annealing because it restores the quality of the material to some extent, although there may be a slight decrease in the tensile strength.
    In order to PROPERLY anneal a chain, it should be heated to a

    A. cherry-red, and quenched in a light grade of oil
    B. straw color, and allowed to cool slowly
    C. straw color, and quenched in a special lime solution
    D. cherry-red, and allowed to cool slowly

13.____

14. In order to hang several pipe lines, it is decided to set expansion shields in masonry walls and ceiling slabs. The tool or device which should be used to bore a hole in the masonry is a

    A. blue point chisel   B. diamond point chisel
    C. star drill   D. round nose drill

14.____

15. Feedwater is delivered to a boiler by means of a line which is approximately 1.5" I.D. In order to deliver twice as much feedwater at the same pipe-flow velocity, the APPROXIMATE I.D. of the line should be

    A. 3.00"   B. 2.12"   C. 1.98"   D. 2.98"

15.____

16. In a steam generating plant, where steam is to be used for both process work and heating, the type of steam trap which can NOT be used to handle large amounts of condensate is the

    A. blast type thermostatic   B. thermostatic
    C. bucket (upright)   D. bucket (inverted)

16.____

17. An inverted bucket-type trap is opened for inspection by a steamfitter. He finds a hole in the top of the bucket. Before closing this trap, he plugs this hole. Thereafter, in operation, this trap will

    A. become steam bound
    B. become air bound
    C. work extremely well
    D. work, but will begin to leak in time

    17.____

18. The MAXIMUM capacity of a combination float and thermostatic trap under given working conditions is dependent entirely upon the

    A. diameter of the float
    B. I.P.S. size of the inlet and outlet connections
    C. free area of the float valve alone
    D. free area of both the float valve and the thermostatic valve

    18.____

19. A combination float and thermostatic trap is to be installed for service with a unit heater. A check on the operation of this equipment shows that it operates at low rates of flow constantly for long periods of time. Under these conditions, the probability is that the float

    A. valve seat will become cut and the trap will leak
    B. valve will remain tight
    C. will finally collapse
    D. will finally pit, fill, and sink

    19.____

20. An IMPORTANT advantage in the operation of a throttling-type trap is that

    A. there are relatively few moving parts in the chamber of the trap
    B. the level of the condensate in the receiving chamber remains constant
    C. it has no moving parts once it is adjusted for a desired flow
    D. it is rarely used with a strainer on the inlet side

    20.____

21. The specifications for a fuel oil piping job for the installation of a storage tank for #6 oil states that a 1" telltale with a swing check is to be installed. This information should indicate that

    A. the length of the fill line is greater than 100'
    B. the vent line does not end within sight of the fill line terminal
    C. the fill line terminal is below the top of the oil storage tank
    D. there is a great possibility that surface water will enter the tank and the telltale will show the presence of this water in the tank

    21.____

22. The specifications for a heavy fuel oil burner job requires the installation of two suction lines (high and low). In order to hold the need for auxiliary equipment to a minimum, these lines should be properly valved and then joined as one suction line AHEAD of the fuel oil

    A. heaters
    B. suction pumps
    C. suction strainers
    D. electric preheaters

    22.____

23. When installing pressure gauges on a steam generating boiler, be sure the siphon loop contains water before connecting the gauge.
The PRIMARY reason for following this advice is to

    A. be able to run the boiler at its proper water level and pressure
    B. keep the bourdon tube in the gauge from coming into direct contact with steam
    C. keep the gauge glass from breaking, should it come into contact with steam
    D. keep soot from sticking to the bourdon tube, especially when blowing soot or lancing the tubes

24. A steam heating system is of the two-pipe up-feed gravity design. The dry return changes to a wet return at its furthest point from the boiler. In operation, there is a difference in pressure of 0.75 lbs. per sq. in. between the boiler and the highest point of wet return. As a result of the above condition, the height of the water leg in the wet return above the boiler water line should be MOST NEARLY _____ ft.

    A. 0.75   B. 1.73   C. 9.00   D. 1.25

25. Forged steel flanges by *Tube-Turn* are manufactured in several types, i.e., *Welding Neck, Screwed, Slip On,* and *Lapped.*
The one type of flange which, during installation of a 10" line, allows the GREATEST ease in lining up is the

    A. Wending Neck   B. Screwed   C. Slip On   D. Lapped

KEY (CORRECT ANSWERS)

1.	C		11.	C
2.	D		12.	C
3.	A		13.	D
4.	B		14.	C
5.	B		15.	B
6.	D		16.	B
7.	D		17.	B
8.	B		18.	D
9.	B		19.	A
10.	A		20.	C

21.	B
22.	C
23.	B
24.	B
25.	D

TEST 2

DIRECTIONS: Each question or incomplete statement is followed by several suggested answers or completions. Select the one that BEST answers the question or completes the statement. *PRINT THE LETTER OF THE CORRECT ANSWER IN THE SPACE AT THE RIGHT.*

1. With respect to seamless steel pipe 10" and smaller, the schedule number which gives MOST NEARLY the same steel pipe wall thickness as standard weight is

    A. 100 B. 80 C. 40 D. 10

2. With respect to welded steel pipe 8" and smaller, the schedule number which gives MOST NEARLY the same steel pipe wall thickness as extra strong is

    A. 10 B. 80 C. 40 D. 100

3. Forged carbon steel flanges are specified in keeping with a primary service (working) pressure rating, i.e., 150 pound, 300 pound, 400 pound, etc. These flange ratings are closely connected to a service temperature (working temperature) when specified for actual use.
   For the 300-pound flange, the service pressure (working pressure) rating is NOT greater than the primary rating when the service temperature (working temperature) is NOT greater than _____ °F.

    A. 750 B. 700 C. 600 D. 300

4. A 6" steam riser covered with standard thickness 85% magnesia is to be installed in a five-story building. The riser pipe is specified as double extra strong (schedule number 120). In order to properly pass this riser through each of the floor slabs, pipe sleeves of standard weight W.I. are to be set.
   To provide for ease of installation and possible slight misalignment from the vertical centerline, the MINIMUM size of pipe to use as a sleeve should be

    A. 7" B. 8" C. 10" D. 12"

5. On many occasions, a set of plans and specifications requires the use of eccentric reducers in a given run of a steam main. The MOST important reason for this is that

    A. pipe supports may be set at a constant elevation
    B. multiple- or gang-type pipe anchors may be used
    C. no pockets are worked into the line to interfere with proper drainage
    D. the line is given an increased springiness in order to take up excessive expansion

6. A low pressure steam manifold is set up to supply steam for heating in a public office building. This manifold supplies steam to four zones, each through a 6" steam line, and each of these lines is equipped with a rising stem flanged steel gate valve. These valves are set so that the stem projects horizontally.
   The MINIMUM clearance (measured from the centerline of the 6" pipe) which must be provided for the proper operation of these valves ranges from

    A. 33 to 50" B. 18 to 34" C. 20 to 30" D. 19 to 31"

7. When installing a run of steam piping, it becomes necessary to offset the line. This offset can be made in any one of several ways with different combinations of fittings.
The combination of fittings which will offer the LEAST resistance to flow is

   A. two 90° standard elbows and a short nipple
   B. two tees and a short nipple, and one run of each tee plugged
   C. a 90° standard elbow and a 90° medium sweep elbow with a nipple
   D. a 90° medium sweep elbow and a 90° long sweep elbow with a nipple

7._____

8. From time to time on various jobs, it becomes necessary to make bends in pipes under field conditions. On one such occasion, when hot-bending a sand-filled welded seam pipe, free hand, it is noted that the pipe stretches, the sand becomes loose, and the pipe flattens slightly. To correct for this flatness, one should

   A. use a low-melting temperature alloy in place of the sand
   B. overbend slightly and open the bend to the required shape
   C. use a rosin in place of the sand
   D. keep the welded seam of the pipe on the outside of the bend

8._____

9. In the course of installing a boiler in a combination power generating station and heating plant, it becomes necessary to bend into shape a hard-drawn copper feed-water line. Prior to making this bend, the steamfitter should

   A. anneal that portion of the copper pipe in which the bend is to be made
   B. fill the pipe with rosin and then bend cold
   C. fill the pipe with tar and then bend cold
   D. heat treat that portion of the pipe in which the bend is to be made to produce a skin hardness

9._____

10. The job plans and specifications required that welded seam steel pipe be used for a given steam line which is to have several long radius bends. These bends are to be fabricated in the field.
When making these bends, the welded seam should be so positioned as to be

    A. on the inside of the bend
    B. on the outside of the bend
    C. on the side of the bend
    D. spiralled around the bend from outside to inside

10._____

11. In the course of piping up a duplex steam-driven boiler feed pump, the steamfitter starts to mate a forged steel narrow raised face flange to the cast iron flange on the pump casing, and uses alloy steel bolts in order to be able to make up this joint tightly.
In this case, the

    A. tightest joint is desirable, and the fitter is doing the right thing
    B. fitter is taking a calculated risk, inasmuch as the steel flange may be warped slightly
    C. fitter should not be allowed to make up this joint in the manner described as he may crack the cast iron flange
    D. fitter should not be allowed to make up this joint in the manner described as he may bend one of the bolts

11._____

12. A safety valve for use with an expansion fluid, such as steam or air, differs from a relief valve in that a safety valve   12.____

    A. may, by code, be used only on unfired pressure vessels
    B. may be set on the job immediately before being installed
    C. has an adjusting, or huddling, ring and chamber to control the amount the pressure blows down before the valve reseats
    D. is made only for service with pressure in excess of 15 lbs.

13. Many surface-type condensers are provided with atmospheric exhaust valves, with piping leading to the atmosphere, to protect the condenser against excess pressure in case there is failure of the condenser circulating water supply. These atmospheric exhaust valves are generally equipped with water sealed seats.   13.____
    This valve is equipped this way in order to

    A. keep the seat from wearing unevenly
    B. prevent air leakage into the condenser when the valve is closed
    C. cool the seat
    D. keep the valve disc from lifting when the condenser is under a vacuum

Questions 14-15.

DIRECTIONS: Questions 14 and 15 are related to the partial specification below. Concerning the globe valves in a certain low pressure steam heating system, the partial specification reads: The disks in all globe valves shall be renewable and shall be of hard rubber composition. All globe valves shall be installed in such a position that, when the valve is closed, the pressure must always be beneath the seat.

14. With this system in operation for several years, it can then be reasonably expected that   14.____

    A. the greater number of the metal valve seats would have to be removed and replaced
    B. the valve stem packing could not be renewed unless the entire system was secured
    C. all of the disks would still be in good condition
    D. some of the valves would leak when closed

15. In connection with this partial specification, it can be said that the   15.____

    A. specified position for valve installation is not good
    B. disk material is acceptable if wet steam does not reach it
    C. disk material is all right if the valve is never used for throttling the flow
    D. disk material is not recommended for this service

Questions 16-20.

DIRECTIONS: Questions 16 through 20, inclusive, are based upon the piping layout given in the figure shown on the following page.

NOTE: 1. All run-outs and returns from radiators to be 1"
2. Return lines at radiators are to be dry return

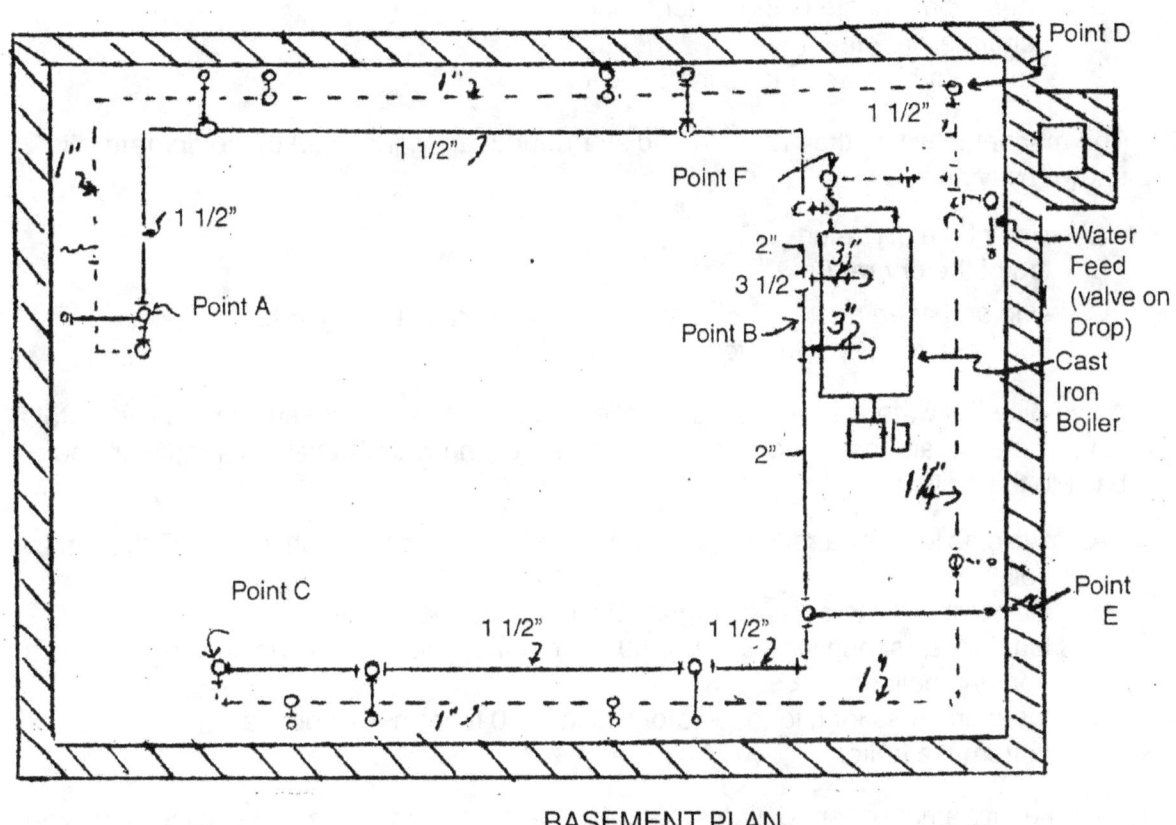

BASEMENT PLAN

PIPING LAYOUT FOR HEATING

NOT TO SCALE

16. A close study of the basement piping layout shows that the heating system is BEST described as a(n)

    A. two-pipe vapor system with a vacuum pump return
    B. up-feed gravity two-pipe system
    C. up-feed two-pipe vapor system with an automatic return trap
    D. down-feed two-pipe gravity system

17. The basement piping (excluding runouts and returns for radiators) should be installed in such a manner that the high point of the piping is Point

    A. B   B. A   C. C   D. D

18. In accordance with this basement plan, the LEAST number of radiators which are to be connected to the piping system shown is

    A. 8   B. 6   C. 4   D. 10

19. If Point F at its highest elevation is 1" above the boiler water line, it can then be said that, in operation, the system will   19._____

    A. not return condensate to the boiler properly
    B. return condensate to the boiler properly
    C. generate wet steam
    D. run with a high water level in the boiler

20. The manner in which the individual radiator returns are connected to the dry return is shown by tying into the   20._____

    A. side of the dry return
    B. top of the dry return
    C. side and at an angle of 45° above the horizontal of the dry return
    D. bottom of the dry return forming a water seal

21. A two-pipe hot water heating job is installed with a reverse return system. In this installation, it can be said that the distance through which the water travels to a radiator and back to the boiler is   21._____

    A. twice as long for a radiator 50 ft. from the boiler as one which is only 25 ft. from the boiler
    B. almost the same distance regardless of radiator locations
    C. four times as long for a radiator 50 ft. from the boiler as one which is only 25 ft. from the boiler
    D. three times as long for a radiator which is 50 ft. from the boiler as one which is 25 ft. from the boiler

22. Assume that a hot water heating system for a large building is being installed. The specified layout shows that the system has been divided into branches or zones. The supply and return for each branch is provided with a gate valve and union.
    Of the following, the BEST reason for the use of these valves and unions is to allow   22._____

    A. use of the valves to control the temperatures of the supply water to the branch
    B. any branch to be drained for repair without taking the entire system out of service
    C. use of the valves and unions when bleeding the system without disturbing the other branches
    D. use and servicing of individual expansion tanks for each branch

23. A hot water heating system is being installed so that it can *float* on the water system from which it is supplied. Only a gate valve and union are installed in the make-up water supply to the heating system. (Assume feedwater pressures to permit the above condition.)
    In connection with this system, a steamfitter should   23._____

    A. install an open-type expansion tank connected to the flow riser
    B. not install an expansion tank
    C. install an open-type expansion tank connected to the return line
    D. install a check valve in addition to the gate valve and union in the feedwater line

24. In a well-installed gravity circulation hot water heating system, the supply mains and branches should pitch up and away from the boiler. Generally, this pitch should be NOT less than _____ ft.

   A. 1" in 10
   B. 1/4" per
   C. 3/4" in 10
   D. 1" in 5

25.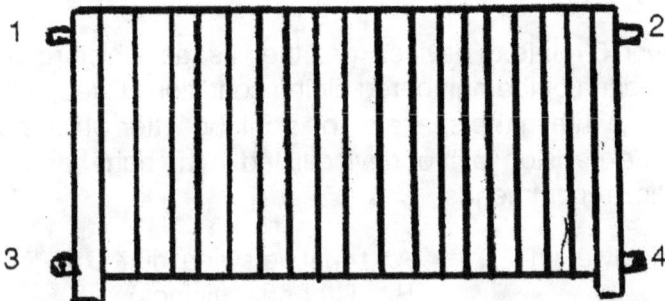

The above sketch shows a hot water radiator and four tapping locations for the supply and return connections.
If this radiator were installed in a forced circulation system, the supply and return connections should be made, respectively, to

   A. 1 and 3
   B. 2 and 4
   C. 4 and 1
   D. 1 and 4

KEY (CORRECT ANSWERS)

1.	C	11.	C
2.	B	12.	C
3.	A	13.	B
4.	C	14.	D
5.	C	15.	D
6.	A	16.	B
7.	D	17.	A
8.	B	18.	B
9.	A	19.	A
10.	C	20.	D

21. B
22. B
23. B
24. A
25. D

TEST 3

DIRECTIONS: Each question or incomplete statement is followed by several suggested answers or completions. Select the one that BEST answers the question or completes the statement. *PRINT THE LETTER OF THE CORRECT ANSWER IN THE SPACE AT THE RIGHT.*

Questions 1-5.

DIRECTIONS: Questions 1 through 5 relate to devices, and their usage, which refer to expansion in piping. For each of the numbered piping conditions listed in the left-hand column below, write in the space at the right the letter which appears in front of the type of expansion joint or device listed in the right-hand column which good practice recommends.

1. Runout and connection to a lightweight convector
2. An outdoor run of a 12" (Sched. 120) high pressure steam line
3. Low pressure steam line in pipe tunnel with limited space and slight misalignment of pipe at joint
4. Low pressure steam line in pipe tunnel with limited space and no misalignment of pipe at joint
5. Radiant heating panel made up of 5/8" type L copper tubing (continuous run)

A. 4-fitting swing joint
B. U-bend (2 fittings)
C. Offset U-bend
D. Slip type expansion joint (no packing)
E. Corrugated bellows type expansion joint
F. 2-fitting rise or drop expansion joint
G. Braided rubber type flexible connection
H. Return bend in piping
J. 45° offset joint

6. Anchors are supports which are fastened rigidly to the pipe to prevent its movement. They are used to locate a given section of pipe positively and to control the direction of the pipe expansion.
It, therefore, follows from the above statement that anchors should

   A. be located near boilers to prevent a thrust or strain on the boiler steam outlet
   B. never be located near boilers because this increases the thrust or strain on the boiler steam outlet
   C. always be located close to both sides of an expansion joint
   D. generally not be located where branches leave the main line

7. A steam main in a heating system is being run a total distance of 75 feet. The specified fall is 1/4" in 10 ft. If the centerline elevation of this main is -10.833' at the beginning of this run, then the centerline elevation at the end of the run is MOST NEARLY

   A. -10.677'   B. -10.989'   C. 12.396'   D. -9.270'

8. Orifice regulating plates are inserted in the valve unions of all radiators to correct for (1) friction loss of pressure in the steam supply piping, (2) extra heat given off in exposed risers and other sources, (3) design errors in the amount or proportioning of radiation, and (4) the filling of radiators at uniform and even rates irrespective of size or location. In the above statement, the number of the statement which is NOT correct is

   A. 3　　　　　B. 2　　　　　C. 4　　　　　D. 1

9. A vapor-type of heating system is being installed in a large apartment house. Because of supply difficulties, the system is installed, in part, without the thermostatic traps at each radiator. The system is then placed in operation. The result of such action would MOST likely be that

   A. the heating capacity of the entire system would be reduced
   B. the system would heat unevenly
   C. control of the system would be simplified in that section which did not have the traps
   D. air removal would be greatly improved in that section which did have the traps

10. The piping of a large heating installation using the vapor system is installed with welded neck flanges.
    The gaskets to be used in the flanged connections should be made of

    A. sheet red rubber　　　　　B. sheet flax
    C. plain stainless steel 18-8　　D. sheet lead

11. A heating system for a given building has been laid out with the use of B & G monoflo fittings. This layout calls for a radiator to be installed below the main. For this radiator, the steamfitter should install

    A. two down feed monoflo fittings directly at the radiator control valves
    B. two down feed monoflo fittings in the branch connections at the main
    C. one down feed monoflo fitting in the supply branch connection at the main
    D. one down feed monoflo fitting in the return branch connection at the main

12. A given hot water heating system, after installation, has the following schedule of piping run sizes and lengths: 4" - 100 ft., 1" - 75 ft., 1 1/2" - 50 ft.
    Assuming that pipe size is I.D. of pipe, the total water storage capacity of all this piping, in gallons, is MOST NEARLY

    A. 9.7　　　　　B. 19.7　　　　　C. 6.7　　　　　D. 12.7

13. In a given hot water heating system, all the radiators are set on the same level as the boiler and the mains are run below the floor. A B&G booster is used to get forced circulation.
    This booster should be installed in the

    A. return line to the boiler from the radiators, and at the boiler
    B. supply line from the boiler to the radiators, and at the boiler
    C. return line to the boiler, and at the point where the compression tank connection is taken
    D. supply line from the boiler, and ahead of the connection to the domestic indirect hot water heater

14. A hot water heating system is installed complete with booster, relief valve, flow control valve, and closed expansion tank. In the course of operation, it develops that there is not enough air space or air cushion to relieve the expansion of the water.
The direct probable result would be that the

    A. booster motor would overheat
    B. flow control valve would not open
    C. compression tank would rupture
    D. relief valve would open and some water would drain from the system

14._____

15. When 25 gallons of water are heated from 40° F to 200° F, the volume of this water increases to 26 gallons.
If the weight of water at 40° F is 8.33 lbs. per gallon, then the weight of water at 200° F is MOST NEARLY _____ lbs. per gallon.

    A. 8.42   B. 8.23   C. 8.02   D. 7.33

15._____

16. A radiator valve is of the packed rising stem type and is used in a vapor heating system. A PRIME advantage in the use of this type of valve is that

    A. regardless of size, the valve is inexpensive
    B. the position of the valve disc can be easily determined
    C. ordinary hemp or oakum is generally recommended as a packing
    D. the valve stem is always made of 18-8 stainless steel.

16._____

17. A high pressure steam line from one of a battery of boilers is provided with a 14" gate valve in the line from this boiler to the boiler room steam manifold. In order that this valve be operated with little difficulty, a steamfitter should install a 2" bypass around the 14" gate valve with a _____ in the bypass.

    A. lift check   B. swing check
    C. locked lift check   D. gate valve

17._____

18. A heating and power steam generating plant is being installed in a building while the building is being erected. Other trades are working in the structure at the same time. It becomes necessary to erect a steam main and its auxiliaries close to ceiling elevation in an area where electricians are completing their work on staging erected for their use. The steamfitters should, upon completion of the electrical work,

    A. wait until the electricians' staging is removed and then erect staging for the steam-fitters' needs
    B. try to get permission to use the electricians' staging as is
    C. use the electricians' staging as is
    D. use the electricians' staging, but first replace the guard rails and toe boards

18._____

19. In the course of erection of a steam main, it becomes necessary for a gang of steamfitters to work directly under an opening in the first floor. Other trades are working on the same floor, as well as on the floors above. Under these conditions,

19._____

A. a watchman should be stationed at the floor opening to warn the steamfitters if any dangerous situation arises
B. a steel reinforced concrete slab should be poured directly over the floor opening, to be removed later if necessary
C. the floor opening should be properly covered with 12" x 2" long leaf yellow pine planking
D. the floor opening should be covered with a tarpaulin properly secured

20. A gang of steamfitters is assigned to make repairs to a steam main in a boiler room. The men are working from a staging 20' above the boiler room floor. While reaching out from this staging, one of the men loses his balance and falls to the floor. When the other men reach him, he appears to be unconscious.
In keeping with established first aid practice, the men should

   A. apply the standard technique of artificial respiration to restore consciousness
   B. cover the man to keep him warm and at the same time send a responsible person to call a doctor
   C. get some brandy and force the unconscious man to drink it while someone is sent to call a doctor
   D. quickly call a taxicab and rush the man to a hospital

21. In a steam-electric power generating plant, it becomes necessary for a gang of steamfitters to make repairs to a high pressure steam line directly over an electric generator. The steamfitters, upon their arrival in the engine room, find this generator in operation and no operating personnel in the engine room.
The steamfitters should

   A. go ahead with their work after having one of their men shut down the engine driving the generator
   B. go ahead with their work after first sending one of their men to look for the operating man in charge
   C. cover the operating generator with a tarpaulin in order to protect it, and then go ahead with their work
   D. wait for the operating man in charge to appear, and arrange for the protection of men and equipment before starting work

22. A heating and ventilating system is installed in an office building with a complete system of pneumatically operated control equipment. The air line for the control of the outside air tempering coils is run directly through the outside air intake duct, ahead of the tempering coils.
The way in which this air piping has been installed may be judged

   A. *very good,* as low outside air temperature acts to reduce the moisture content of the compressed air in this line
   B. *acceptable,* if the controller is of the *leak-stat type*
   C. *poor,* as in very cold weather the outside air will freeze any moisture in the compressed air line and the controls will not work properly
   D. *poor,* as it will greatly increase the resistance to air flow in this outside air intake duct

23. A condensate return system is so installed as to provide for the direct return of condensate to the boiler by means of a high level receiver and a three-valve lifting trap of the tilting type.
The recommended position of this lifting trap with respect to the boiler water line, when the boiler is operating at 30 lbs, per sq.in., is MOST NEARLY _____ the water line.

    A. 3 ft. above
    B. 2 ft. above
    C. 2'6" above
    D. 2" below

24. A steamfitter was on a construction job along with the journeymen of other trades. He stepped on a board that had a nail sticking out of it. The nail went through the thin sole of his shoe and into his left foot. He was wearing ordinary shoes and they were not new. In keeping with good safety practices for construction work, the steamfitter should be

    A. laid off, as he is a compensation risk
    B. directed to buy a pair of safety shoes which are to be worn at all times
    C. told to have his eyes examined by a doctor and follow his recommendations at once
    D. told not to wander around the construction job

25. In a comparison of the specifications for threaded and unthreaded brass pipe, it can be CORRECTLY stated that

    A. size for size, the wall thickness of the unthreaded pipe is generally less than that of the threaded pipe
    B. the minimum copper content of the threaded pipe is generally greater
    C. the unthreaded pipe, though intended for use with approved silver-brazed joints, may be threaded and properly used with threaded fittings
    D. size for size, the weight per linear foot is the same for both threaded and unthreaded pipe

KEY (CORRECT ANSWERS)

1. A
2. C
3. E
4. E
5. H

6. A
7. B
8. C
9. B
10. A

11. B
12. A
13. B
14. D
15. C

16. B
17. D
18. A
19. C
20. B

21. D
22. C
23. A
24. B
25. A

———

EXAMINATION SECTION
TEST 1

DIRECTIONS: Each question or incomplete statement is followed by several suggested answers or completions. Select the one that BEST answers the question or completes the statement. *PRINT THE LETTER OF THE CORRECT ANSWER IN THE SPACE AT THE RIGHT.*

1. Cast-iron heating boilers that are shipped in sections are USUALLY assembled on the job location with

    A. stud bolts and nuts
    B. push nipples and tie rods
    C. anchor bolts
    D. stay bolts

    1._____

2. In a two-pipe mechanical condensate-return system, the two valves that are installed in the discharge piping between the condensate pump and boiler are a _____ valve and _____ check valve.

    A. gate; swing
    B. globe; lift
    C. gate; lift
    D. globe; swing

    2._____

3. When a thermostatic trap is used in a steam supply heating system, the *cooling leg* must be installed

    A. between the equipment or drip and the thermostatic trap
    B. after the thermostatic trap
    C. at an angle of 45° to the main
    D. below the water line of the boiler

    3._____

4. The essential features of construction of a Hartford Loop connection to a steam heating boiler are a direct connection between the steam side and return side of the boiler and a _____ from the return main to the return side of the boiler.

    A. long nipple connection two inches above the normal water line
    B. close nipple connection two inches below the normal water line
    C. valved (gate) connection
    D. connection at the water level

    4._____

5. *Unit trapping* of two or more steam-consuming condensing units is recommended to

    A. allow for expansion of pipes
    B. eliminate check valves
    C. prevent the build-up of condensate and air in one or more units
    D. increase the back pressure on each unit

    5._____

6. Packless type steam radiator supply valves are recommended for use in _____ heating systems.

    A. two-pipe vacuum
    B. two-pipe vapor
    C. one-pipe gravity air-vent
    D. two-pipe gravity air-vent

    6._____

19

7. Of the following types of high-pressure steam piping systems, the one which is WIDELY used in small and medium-sized plants is the _____ system.

   A. single-header B. spider
   C. loop or ring D. unit

8. Compressed-air systems in power plants USUALLY operate at pressures of _____ psig.

   A. 30 to 40 B. 50 to 60 C. 70 to 90 D. 100 to 125

9. A *return header* is used on a cast-iron sectional boiler to distribute the condensate to both rear tappings.
   Of the following fittings, the ones that should be used where the branch connections enter the return tappings are

   A. elbows B. full size plugged tees
   C. reducer couplings D. bull head tees

10. The MINIMUM pitch for horizontal runouts to risers and heating units in a two-pipe high-pressure steam system should be

    A. 1/4 inch in 10 feet B. 1/8 inch per foot
    C. 1/4 inch per foot D. 1/2 inch per foot

11. The air suction intake of an air compressor has to be relocated 30 feet further from the compressor than present location.
    In connection with this work, it would be recommended practice to

    A. install a drip at mid-point of the extended suction line
    B. increase the capacity of the air storage tank
    C. increase the diameter of the suction line piping
    D. install a relief valve immediately before the intake of the air compressor

12. Of the following statements pertaining to steam-supplied blast heaters, the one which is INCORRECT is that

    A. steam mains should be dripped into the heater sections
    B. return piping from heater to trap should be of the same size as the heater outlet connection
    C. return piping should not be run to an overhead main which is above the heater return connection
    D. steam piping and heater sections should be supported independently

13. A hot water heating line has to be offset to clearn an obstruction.
    Of the following combinations of fittings, the one which will offer the LEAST resistance to the flow of hot water is

    A. two 90° standard elbows and a short nipple
    B. two tees, with one run of each tee plugged, and a short nipple
    C. a 90° standard elbow, a 90° long turn elbow, and a short nipple
    D. two 90° long turn elbows and a short nipple

14. The inlet piping to each heating unit in a two-pipe vapor steam heating system should be equipped with a(n) _____ valve.   14._____

    A. gate   B. modulating
    C. OS & Y   D. check

15. Of the following piping materials, the one that should NOT be used in a fuel-oil piping system is   15._____

    A. steel pipe   B. brass pipe
    C. type K copper tubing   D. galvanized iron

16. Assume that a shut-off valve is installed in the discharge line from an oil pump. In this installation, the valve that should be installed between the oil pump and the shut-off valve is a _____ valve.   16._____

    A. swing check   B. globe
    C. relief   D. air

17. A pump is to be raised 1/2" above its bed-plate. One 1/4" plate and one 3/16" plate are used.
    The number of 1/64" shims that must be used in addition to the 1/4" and 3/16" plates is   17._____

    A. 4   B. 7   C. 11   D. 20

18. If 250 feet of 4" pipe weighs 400 pounds, the weight of this pipe per linear foot is _____ pounds.   18._____

    A. 1.25   B. 1.50   C. 1.60   D. 1.75

19. The proper designation for a tee fitting which has on the *run* a 1 1/2" pipe thread and a 2" pipe thread with the *branch* having a 1" pipe thread is   19._____

    A. 1" x 1 1/2" x 2"   B. 1 1/2" x 1" x 2"
    C. 2" x 1" x 1 1/2"   D. 2" x 1 1/2" x 1"

20. Taper-tapped couplings are recommended for _____ piping.   20._____

    A. low-pressure gas   B. high-pressure steam
    C. vent   D. potable water supply

21. A steam heating system that operates both in vacuum and under low-pressure (0 to 15 psig) conditions without the use of a vacuum pump is known as a _____ system.   21._____

    A. high-pressure   B. low-pressure
    C. vapor   D. vacuum

22. A flange joint in a high-temperature piping system has to be broken frequently. To prevent the gasket from sticking to the flange face, it is GOOD practice to coat the gasket with   22._____

    A. high-grade epoxy   B. water-resistant grease
    C. graphite   D. talc

23. Pipe dope is applied to the male threads and not to the female threads when making-up a screwed pipe joint. The MAIN reason for this is to   23._____

    A. compensate for not using wicking
    B. prevent contamination of the fluid in the piping system

C. save on pipe dope material and labor
D. reduce friction when pulling-up the joint

24. Flanged faces of steel valves and fittings are NORMALLY manufactured with _____ flange face(s).

   A. raised
   B. plain
   C. flat
   D. one end having a raised flange face and the other end a plain

25. Regulating or throttling valves are SELDOM used in sizes above

   A. 12"   B. 15"   C. 18"   D. 20"

26. An 80' steam heating main is being piped up.
    If the pitch (fall) is 1/4" in 10 feet, and the centerline elevation at the beginning of the run is 9.989 feet, then the centerline elevation, in feet, at the lower end of the run is MOST NEARLY

   A. 11.989   B. 10.156   C. 9.822   D. 7.989

27. A set of heating plan drawings is drawn to a scale of 1/4" = 1 foot.
    If a length of pipe measures 4 5/8" on the drawing, the actual length of the pipe, in feet, is

   A. 16.3   B. 16.8   C. 17.5   D. 18.5

28. Of the following pastes, the one which is NOT suitable for making up threads in oil piping is

   A. red glyptol
   B. litharge and glycerin
   C. white or red lead oil paste
   D. permatex

29. Of the following valves, the one which is used for preventing the reversal of flow in a pipe is the _____ valve.

   A. check   B. globe
   C. pressure-regulating D. gate

30. Of the following fittings, the one that is used to connect a 1 1/4" pipe directly to a 1" pipe in a straight line is called a

   A. union   B. sleeve   C. reducer   D. nipple

31. The pipe diameter of header drips installed in a high-pressure steam piping system USUALLY ranges from

   A. 1/4" to 1/2"   B. 3/4" to 1"
   C. 1 1/2" to 1 3/4"   D. 2" to 2 1/2"

32. Of the following types of gasket material, the types that should be used between flanges on a pipe conveying 900° F hot water is

    A. red rubber or neoprene
    B. fiber or paper
    C. copper, corrugated or plain
    D. steel, corrugated or plain

33. The MAIN reason for installing a by-pass line around a 10" high-pressure gate valve is to

    A. make it easier to close the valve
    B. make it easier to open the valve
    C. reduce the steam-line pressure
    D. tap off steam for other uses

34. Of the following valves, the one that is considered a *dead end* type of valve is a _____ valve.

    A. single-seated pressure-reducing
    B. double-seated pressure-reducing
    C. high-pressure steam-throttling
    D. relief

35. A valve is marked *600 WOG*.
    This valve could NOT be properly used in a pipe conveying _____ pounds gage maximum.

    A. water at 500
    B. oil at 600
    C. air at 300
    D. steam at 600

36. Flange dimensions and materials are established by the

    A. ASA (American Standards Association) *Code for Pressure Piping*
    B. ASME (American Society of Mechanical Engineers) *Boiler Code*
    C. NDHA (National District Heating Association) *Piping Code*
    D. NBS (National Bureau of Standards) *Piping Materials Code*

37. A steam leak in a pipe line allows steam to escape at a rate of 50,000 pounds each month.
    Assuming that the cost of steam is 50 cents per 1,000 pounds, the total cost of wasted steam from this leak for a 12-month period would amount to

    A. $25   B. $60   C. $300   D. $600

38. Of the following, the method which is MOST likely to give an accurate reading in checking a 0-to-400 psig pressure gage is to

    A. adjust the pointer to zero
    B. connect the gage and a *test gage* to a pressure line in which the pressures may be varied, and compare the readings of the two gages
    C. use a dead-weight gage tester
    D. connect the gage to a steam line and compare the pressure reading with another gage installed on the same steam line

39. An oil separator in a non-condensing steam plant removes oil from

   A. live steam
   B. feedwater
   C. exhaust steam
   D. condensate

40. The MAIN function of a double offset U-bend in a high-pressure steam line is to

   A. protect pressure gages
   B. reverse the steam flow
   C. permit expansion of the steam line
   D. by-pass a trap or valve

KEY (CORRECT ANSWERS)

1. B	11. C	21. C	31. B
2. A	12. A	22. C	32. D
3. A	13. D	23. B	33. B
4. B	14. B	24. A	34. A
5. C	15. D	25. A	35. D
6. A	16. C	26. C	36. A
7. A	17. A	27. D	37. C
8. D	18. C	28. C	38. C
9. B	19. D	29. A	39. C
10. D	20. B	30. C	40. C

TEST 2

DIRECTIONS: Each question or incomplete statement is followed by several suggested answers or completions. Select the one that BEST answers the question or completes the statement. *PRINT THE LETTER OF THE CORRECT ANSWER IN THE SPACE AT THE RIGHT.*

1. The MINIMUM permitted diameter of the pipes connecting a water column to a power boiler is

    A. 1/4"   B. 3/8"   C. 3/4"   D. 1"

    1._____

2. A steam gage is installed above a steam pipe with a gooseneck siphon. The MAIN purpose of the gooseneck siphon is to

    A. maintain a water seal between the gage and steam supply
    B. drip condensate back into the steam pipeline
    C. allow for expansion of the connection
    D. eliminate vibrations

    2._____

3. The anemometer rating of a unit ventilator is USUALLY expressed in

    A. pounds per square inch   B. cubic feet per minute
    C. BTU/hour   D. pounds per hour

    3._____

4. In accordance with the ASME Code for Low Pressure Heating Boilers, the MAXIMUM allowable working pressure for a hot water heating boiler is _____ psi.

    A. 15   B. 30   C. 160   D. 250

    4._____

5. The MOST common device used for measuring steam consumption in a district heating system is the

    A. steam flow meter   B. condensate meter
    C. Bailey meter   D. manometer

    5._____

6. Of the following types of steam traps, the one which must be primed or filled with water prior to operation is the _____ trap.

    A. inverted-bucket   B. open or upright-bucket
    C. float   D. float-and-thermostatic

    6._____

7. Of the following types of steam traps, the one which is recommended for dripping the ends of steam mains is the _____ trap.

    A. float   B. inverted-bucket
    C. open or upright-bucket   D. float-and-thermostatic

    7._____

8. The removal of carbon dioxide gas from a two-pipe system heating system is accomplished by the use of a

    A. blow-off connection on the boiler
    B. steam trap
    C. steam separator
    D. relief valve

    8._____

25

9. In a true packless-type steam radiator supply valve, leakage around the stem is prevented by a

   A. regular packing nut
   B. diaphragm
   C. metal bellows
   D. packing gland

10. Of the following types of steam radiator supply valves, the one MOST generally used in a two-pipe steam heating system is the _____ type.

    A. straightway
    B. right-hand
    C. angle
    D. left-hand

11. The MAIN function of a *Copes Regulator* is to regulate the amount of

    A. steam leaving a boiler
    B. feedwater entering a boiler drum
    C. make up water leaving the closed feedwater heater
    D. steam pressure in a boiler drum

12. A device that could be used in a low-pressure hot water system which would help prevent air from entering the main is the

    A. relief valve
    B. dip tube
    C. circulating pump
    D. flow-check valve

13. The function of an *injector* in a steam plant is to

    A. supply fuel oil to the burners
    B. spray water into the hot well
    C. drain the after cooler
    D. lift and force water into a boiler

14. Of the following knots, the one that is used to take the strain off the connections to an electrical plug is the

    A. square knot
    B. underwriter's knot
    C. clove hitch
    D. slip knot

15. The safety term *safe-ending* pertains MOST NEARLY to

    A. hammer-struck tools such as chisels or number dies
    B. circular saw blades
    C. large pipe wrenches
    D. pipe dies and reamers

16. Of the following types of portable fire extinguishers, the one which should be used on a *live* electrical fire is the _____ type.

    A. foam
    B. carbon dioxide
    C. soda-acid
    D. water

17. The MAIN reason for using a three-pronged plug with portable electrical tools is to

    A. decrease the amperage rating of the fuse
    B. provide a means to conserve electrical energy
    C. increase the line voltage
    D. ground them properly

18. The total length of four pieces of pipe whose lengths are 3 ft. 4 1/2 in., 2 ft. 1 5/16 in., 4 ft. 9 3/8 in., and 2 ft. 3 1/4 in., respectively, is   18._____

    A. 11 ft. 5 7/16"   B. 11 ft. 6 7/16"
    C. 12 ft. 5 7/16"   D. 12 ft. 6 7/16"

19. The DESIRABLE feature of a ratchet wrench is that it   19._____

    A. can exert more force than an open-end wrench
    B. does not damage the nut
    C. can be used in a limited space without removing the wrench from the nut
    D. will not strip the threads

20. A drift punch is used to   20._____

    A. tighten small rivets
    B. set escutcheon pin heads
    C. enlarge small holes
    D. drive out pins

21. Of the following tools, the one which it is BEST to use to remove burrs from the inside of a pipe is a(n)   21._____

    A. auger bit   B. diamond-point chisel
    C. pillar file   D. reamer

22. The tool or device which should be used to bore a hole in a concrete wall is a   22._____

    A. round-nose drill   B. diamond-point chisel
    C. center punch   D. star drill

23. Of the following wrenches, the one which is the MOST suitable and fastest to work with when pulling up flange bolts and nuts is a(n) _____ wrench.   23._____

    A. open-end or socket   B. monkey or hex
    C. pipe   D. chain pipe

24. Assume that a pipe threading die has a set of 4 chasers and the heel clearance of the chaser threads is worn away.   24._____
    Of the following actions, the BEST one to take would be to have the

    A. lip rake angle re-ground
    B. cutting angle re-ground
    C. lead angle beveled
    D. set replaced

25. Of the following sizes of pipe wrenches, the one that is GENERALLY used to make up 3/4" or 1" diameter pipe is   25._____

    A. 18"   B. 10"   C. 8"   D. 6"

26. A 1:3:5 concrete mix is a mixture consisting of 1 part _____, 3 parts _____, and 5 parts _____.   26._____

    A. gravel, cement, sand   B. cement, sand, gravel
    C. gravel, sand, cement   D. sand, cement, gravel

Questions 27-31.

DIRECTIONS: Questions 27 through 31, inclusive, are to be answered in accordance with the American Standard Graphical Symbols for Pipe Fittings, Valves, and Piping.

27. The graphical symbol —//——//——//— drawn on a heating plan represents a

    A. boiler blow-off
    B. high-pressure steam
    C. make-up water
    D. low-pressure return

28. The graphical symbol ——⋈—— drawn on a heating plan represents a _____ globe valve.

    A. flanged
    B. screwed
    C. bell-and-spigot
    D. welded

29. The graphical symbol ——▭—— drawn on a heating plan represents a _____ trap

    A. boiler return
    B. thermostatic
    C. float
    D. float and thermostatic

30. The graphical symbol ——✕ᴴ—— drawn on a heating plan represents a(n)

    A. anchor
    B. hot well
    C. support or hanger
    D. heater

31. The graphical symbol ——Ⓓ→ drawn on a heating plan represents a(n) _____ pump.

    A. condensate
    B. circulating water
    C. reciprocating
    D. air

32. In the sketch shown at the right, if the constant for the 30° angle is equal to 2,000 and the A dimension is equal to 6, then X is equal to

    A. 12
    B. 8
    C. 3
    D. 1/3

33. Assume that a pipe trench is 3 feet wide, 3 feet deep, and 300 feet long. If the unit cost of excavating the trench is $40 per cubic yard, the total cost of excavating the trench is

    A. $400
    B. $4,000
    C. $9,000
    D. $12,000

5 (#2)

Questions 34-36.

DIRECTIONS: Questions 34 through 36, inclusive, are to be answered in accordance with the following par

The heat output from unit heaters will depend on how fast and how completely dry hot steam fills the unit core. For complete and fast air removal and rapid drainage of condensate, use a trap actuated by water or vapor (inverted bucket trap) .and not a trap operated by temperature only (thermostatic or bellows trap). A temperature-actuated trap will hold back the hot condensate until it cools to a point where the thermal element opens. When this happens,, the condensate backs up in the heater and reduces the heat output. With a water-actuated trap, this will not happen, as the water or condensate is discharged as fast as it is formed.

34. On the basis of the information given in the above paragraph, it can be concluded that the proper type of trap to use for a unit heater is a(n) _____ trap.   34._____

    A. thermostatic
    B. bellows-type
    C. inverted bucket
    D. temperature

35. According to the above paragraph, the MAIN reason for using the type of trap specified for a unit heater is to   35._____

    A. bring the condensate up to steam temperature
    B. prevent reduction in the heat output of the unit heater
    C. permit cycling of the heater
    D. maintain constant temperature of condensate in the trap

36. As used in the above paragraph, the word *actuated* means MOST NEARLY   36._____

    A. clogged   B. operated   C. cleaned   D. vented

37. When supervising a helper, you should be   37._____

    A. fair in your actions towards him
    B. stern and to the point
    C. apologetic and condescending
    D. sarcastic and smart

38. Assume that a helper under your supervision disagrees with your evaluation of his work. Of the following statements, the one which describes the BEST way to handle the situation is to   38._____

    A. refuse to discuss his contention in order to maintain discipline
    B. advise him that the other men are satisfied with your evaluation and he has no right to complain
    C. explain to him that since you have more working experience, you are more able to evaluate his work than he is
    D. explain the basis of your evaluation and discuss it with him

39. The MAIN responsibility of anyone who has men working under him is to

    A. make himself liked and respected by his men.
    B. see that all his men are treated the same when duties are assigned
    C. create an attitude in his men which will be receptive toward policies of the department
    D. get the work done properly

40. The BEST way of giving directions to a helper, is to

    A. lay out a rough plan of procedure and see if the helper has the intelligence to work out his own method
    B. give only general hints of how you want the work accomplished
    C. be exact and omit none of the essential points
    D. question the helper frequently to determine if he thinks that you have given him sufficient information

KEY (CORRECT ANSWERS)

1.	D	11.	B	21.	D	31.	A
2.	A	12.	B	22.	D	32.	A
3.	B	13.	D	23.	A	33.	B
4.	C	14.	B	24.	D	34.	C
5.	B	15.	A	25.	A	35.	B
6.	A	16.	B	26.	B	36.	B
7.	D	17.	D	27.	B	37.	A
8.	B	18.	D	28.	B	38.	D
9.	C	19.	C	29.	D	39.	D
10.	C	20.	D	30.	C	40.	C

EXAMINATION SECTION
TEST 1

DIRECTIONS: Each question consists of a statement. You are to indicate whether the statement is TRUE (T) or FALSE (F). *PRINT THE LETTER OF THE CORRECT ANSWER IN THE SPACE AT THE RIGHT.*

1. For throttling purposes, the hand operated gate valve is recommended for use over the globe valve. 1.____

2. The globe valve, when fully open, has the same resistance to flow as a gate valve that is 60% closed. 2.____

3. To fully open a globe valve, the disc need only be lifted to 25% of the pipe diameter. 3.____

4. The lift check valve can be of a horizontal or vertical type. 4.____

5. Where rapidly pulsating flow is encountered, and a check valve is required, good practice is to use a swing check valve. 5.____

6. Leather disc swing check valves are NOT recommended specifically for cold water service, especially when foreign matter is present. 6.____

7. For low pressure air service, lift check valves with soft discs are better than metal disc valves. 7.____

8. The abbreviation (Mbh) which is often given in the rating of a low pressure heating boiler stands for *maximum boiler horsepower.* 8.____

9. Frictional losses in a heating system due to tees, elbows, valves, and other fittings are usually expressed in *pipe equivalents* or lineal feet of piping. 9.____

10. In the last 5 years, the average seasonal total number of degree days for the heating season for the city was between 4800 and 5300. 10.____

11. If the highest temperature recorded in the city on November 30th was 50° F and the minimum was 32° F, the number of degree-days for that day was 52. 11.____

12. The outside design temperature that is used in computing the seasonal heat loss for a building in the city is usually 32° F. 12.____

13. Complete stoppage of flow of a liquid in a pipe line is NOT necessary to produce water hammer. 13.____

14. The number of tapered pipe threads per inch in a 3" diameter pipe (American Standard) is usually 8. 14.____

15. In a weight-loaded type of pressure reducing valve, the high pressure side of the system governs the operation of the valve by its action upon the valve diaphragm. 15.____

16. Normally, the weight on a weighted pressure reducing valve lever holds the valve closed. 16.____

17. In a weight-loaded type of pressure reducing valve, the diaphragm control pipe should be connected to the bottom of the steam main, NEVER into the side.   17._____

18. A globe valve should NOT be used in a horizontal condensate return line unless the valve stem is in a vertical position.   18._____

19. The abbreviation (SBI) stands for *steam boiler institute*.   19._____

20. A steel pipe main was installed when the temperature was 60° F and measured 100 feet long. If the expansion of steel is 0.0075 feet per degree rise in temperature, the length of this main when carrying 200° water will MOST likely be approximately 101.07 feet.   20._____

21. When runouts are taken from the top of a steam heating main, it is good practice to use concentric reducing couplings when changing the size of the main.   21._____

22. In a vacuum return steam heating system, it is good practice to pitch all horizontal steam runouts to undripped risers at a slope of not more than 1/2 inch per foot.   22._____

23. When a reduction of steam pressure is made in 2 stages, the pressure reducing valves should NOT be installed more than 20 feet apart.   23._____

24. The bypass line that is customarily used around a pressure reducing valve should NEVER be made smaller in size than the reducing valve size.   24._____

25. The length of thread on a 3" diameter pipe that is screwed into a fitting or valve to make a tight joint should be about 1 inch.   25._____

KEY (CORRECT ANSWERS)

1.	F	11.	F
2.	T	12.	F
3.	T	13.	T
4.	T	14.	T
5.	F	15.	F
6.	F	16.	F
7.	T	17.	F
8.	F	18.	F
9.	T	19.	F
10.	T	20.	T

21.	F
22.	F
23.	F
24.	F
25.	T

TEST 2

DIRECTIONS: Each question consists of a statement. You are to indicate whether the statement is TRUE (T) or FALSE (F). *PRINT THE LETTER OF THE CORRECT ANSWER IN THE SPACE AT THE RIGHT.*

1. Since a condensate pump and a vacuum pump accomplish practically the same thing, they can be interchanged with very few alterations to the condensate return line. 1.____

2. If a 2" diameter pipe discharges 20 gallons of fluid per minute, a 4" diameter pipe under similar conditions (such as internal friction and pressure head) would discharge APPROXIMATELY 64 gallons of fluid per minute. 2.____

3. If a 2" diameter pipe handling 30 gallons of fluid per minute develops a friction head of 40 feet, then 60 gallons of fluid per minute through this same pipe will develop a friction head of 80 feet. 3.____

4. In reference to copper tubing which is sometimes used in heating installations, the designation of a type, such as *Type K,* is sometimes used. This designation of type, merely, is an indication of whether the tubing is of a hard or soft temper. 4.____

5. The outside diameter of copper tubing is always 1/8" larger than the nominal size of all types and sizes of tubing. 5.____

6. Copper tube soldered joints that are made with 95-5 tin-antimony solder can withstand greater internal pressures than a similar joint made with 50-50 tin-lead solder. 6.____

7. Type K copper tubing will offer a lower pressure loss due to friction, in lbs. per sq. in. per 100 ft., than the same size Type L copper tubing handling the same flow of fluid in gallons per minute. 7.____

8. Where a pressure reducing valve assembly is used to obtain low pressure steam for heating purposes, the size of the pipe on the L.P. side of the reducing valve should be smaller than the high side because of a reduction in steam pressure. 8.____

9. The installation of a feeder valve between a high pressure unit heater, sterilizer, cooking kettle or other industrial equipment using high pressure steam, and the high pressure steam trap, is NOT recommended. 9.____

10. A horizontal tank with a semi-circular top and bottom measures internally 10' long x 4' wide and 6' from top to bottom. If this tank is filled with water to a height of 4' from the bottom, it will hold approximately 1070 gallons. 10.____

11. The function of the flux that is used when soldering joints in copper tubing is to clean the copper. 11.____

12. Where an expansion loop is used to take care of the expansion of a steam riser, it is good practice to anchor the loop close to the riser. 12.____

13. Where an expansion joint is to be used on a steam main and this joint is to be located in an inaccessible location, it is good policy to use a packed type joint. 13.____

14. A 45° offset is to be put into a 2" low pressure vertical steam line. This offset is to be 20". With a 2" allowance for fittings, the actual length of pipe that must be cut is 26". 14._____

15. Steam supply springpieces, connecting horizontal L.P. heating mains to upfeed risers, should NEVER be of a larger size than the riser. 15._____

16. One of the functions of a vacuum pump is to remove air and condensable gases from a vacuum steam heating system. 16._____

17. In the Hartford loop method of connecting condensate returns to a boiler, the short nipple connecting the returns to the equalizing line should NEVER be more than 4" below boiler water line. 17._____

18. Where 2 or more L.P. steam heating boilers are connected in a battery, it is NOT necessary that Hartford loop connections or check valves be used in the condensate return connections to the boilers. 18._____

19. The outside diameter of a 4" pipe diameter, class 250, cast iron flange, is 9". 19._____

20. The diameter of the bolts that are used on a standard class 125, 4" pipe flange, is 3/4". 20._____

KEY (CORRECT ANSWERS)

1.	F	11.	F
2.	F	12.	F
3.	F	13.	F
4.	F	14.	F
5.	T	15.	F
6.	T	16.	T
7.	F	17.	T
8.	F	18.	F
9.	F	19.	F
10.	T	20.	F

EXAMINATION SECTION
TEST 1

DIRECTIONS: Each question consists of a statement. You are to indicate whether the statement is TRUE (T) or FALSE (F). *PRINT THE LETTER OF THE CORRECT ANSWER IN THE SPACE AT THE RIGHT.*

1. The number of bolts used in a standard class 125, 3" pipe diameter companion flange is 4.   1.____

2. A pump is said to develop a pressure head of 8 feet of water. This is equivalent to a pressure of 18.4 lbs. per sq. in.   2.____

3. One of the principal uses of the *degree-day* is in predicting fuel consumption for a particular building for a particular period.   3.____

4. The capacity or size of many L.P. heating boilers is rated on a net (I.B.R.) rating. The abbreviation I.B.R. stands for *industrial boiler rating*.   4.____

5. A particular vacuum pump maintains a vacuum of 5 1/2 inches of mercury in the condensate return line. This is equivalent to a *negative* pressure of 2.37 lbs. per sq. in.   5.____

6. It is considered GOOD practice to run the condensate from a high pressure drip trap directly to the vacuum return line leading to the vacuum pump.   6.____

7. In the average vacuum heating system, the vacuum pump is controlled by a vacuum regulator and a float control.   7.____

8. It is generally considered POOR practice to exceed a 2-ounce pressure drop per 100 feet of equivalent run of an L.P. steam main in a vacuum return steam heating system.   8.____

9. The operating principle of the *upright bucket* trap and the *inverted bucket* trap is the same.   9.____

10. The proper installation of an inverted bucket trap, in clearing H.P. steam lines and heating appliances of condensate, should include installation of AT LEAST 2 gate valves and a strainer.   10.____

11. It is good practice to pitch L.P. steam heating mains *not less than* 1 inch in 40 feet.   11.____

12. If a steam main, 120 ft. long, is run with a pitch of 3/8" in 10 feet and the high point of the main is at an elevation of +1.250' in order to clear the soffit of the floor beams, the elevation of the top of the other end of the main will be *approximately* +0.875'.   12.____

13. The proper type of trap to use in draining the condensate from high pressure blast coils and heaters is a float and hydrostatic trap.   13.____

14. A closed float trap is the *appropriate* type of trap to use to drain low pressure steam mains at points where the main rises or where condensate only is to be handled.   14.____

15. In selecting the proper size of pressure reducing valve to use, it is BEST to choose a larger-size valve than a smaller one, where the final pressure is less than 58% of initial pressure.   15.____

16. Schedule 40 steel pipe has the same physical dimensions as double extra heavy pipe. 16._____

17. An oxy-acetylene torch is often used in cutting out existing steel pipe when making repairs. In using this equipment, one should *always* set the oxygen pressure higher than the acetylene pressure. 17._____

18. When selecting a tip for an oxy-acetylene cutting torch, a *good* rule of thumb is to select a higher numbered tip for burning lighter gauge metal. 18._____

19. If a fitter wants to drill and tap a casting to tie in a 3/4" line, he should FIRST use a 3/4" drill or hole cutter in order to get a full thread. 19._____

20. In general, heating distribution systems which take their supply from the exhausts of non-condensing steam engines are *high pressure* systems. 20._____

21. Oil heaters (steam) and oil starting heaters (electric) are *usually* installed with fixed relief valves. 21._____

Questions 22-25.

DIRECTIONS: Questions 22 through 25, inclusive, are to be answered in accordance with the following paragraph.

In district heating work for the distribution of steam, the pressure at which the steam is to be distributed will depend upon (1) boiler pressure, (2) whether exhaust or live steam, (3) pressure requirements of apparatus to be served. If steam has been passed through electrical generating units, the pressure will be considerably lower than if live steam, direct from the boiler, is used. The advantages of low pressure distribution (2 to 30 psi) are (1) smaller heat loss per square foot of pipe surface, (2) less trouble with traps and valves, (3) simpler problems in pressure reduction at the building, and (4) general reduction in maintenance costs. The advantages of high pressure distribution are (1) smaller pipe sizes, (2) greater adaptability, (3) wider flexibility.

22. With reference to the above paragraph, the heat loss per square foot of pipe surface is *inversely proportional* to the steam pressure. 22._____

23. With reference to the above paragraph, high pressure systems have a *lower* maintenance cost than low pressure systems. 23._____

24. The distribution system which should have a *lower* trap maintenance charge is the high pressure system. 24._____

25. The distribution system which must use comparatively *larger* pipe sizes is the lower pressure system. 25._____

KEY (CORRECT ANSWERS)

1. T
2. F
3. T
4. F
5. F

6. F
7. T
8. T
9. F
10. T

11. T
12. T
13. F
14. T
15. F

16. F
17. T
18. F
19. F
20. F

21. T
22. F
23. F
24. F
25. T

TEST 2

DIRECTIONS: Each question consists of a statement. You are to indicate whether the statement is TRUE (T) or FALSE (F). *PRINT THE LETTER OF THE CORRECT ANSWER IN THE SPACE AT THE RIGHT.*

1. A mechanical pressure atomizing type fuel oil burner uses No. 6 fuel oil. The fuel oil pump for this burner should deliver oil at a pressure of 75 lbs. per sq. in.

   1.____

2. In an entire fuel oil piping system for units designed to burn No. 6 oil, only a *single* set of duplex straiters need be furnished and piped between the oil pump and oil heaters, in keeping with good practice.

   2.____

3. In the city, steam heating plants operating in excess of 10 lbs. per sq. in. are considered high pressure plants for purposes of boiler inspection.

   3.____

4. An apprentice receiving a salary of $36 for 5 1/3 hours on the job receives $6 3/4 per hour.

   4.____

5. Considering that cutting consumes 1 1/2" of material, the length of 3/4" brass pipe required to make 12 nipples each 4 1/2" long is 60".

   5.____

6. If the condensate in a return pipe flows at an average rate of 13 gal/hr. for 9 hours per day, then 351 gallons will flow in 3 days.

   6.____

7. Four steamfitters worked on one job. In order to complete this job, each put in the following number of hours: 1st man - 6 1/2 hours, 2nd man - 5 3/4 hours, 3rd man - 7 1/4 hours, 4th man - 6 3/4 hours.
   The total number of hours put in by the men is 25 1/4.

   7.____

8. Assume that the formula to find the amount of water a pump will deliver is:
   $G = D^2 \times C \times S \times N \times T$, where
   - G - Gallons pumped per hour
   - D - Diameter of pump cylinder in inches
   - C - .0408 (contents of 1" cylinder 1 foot long)
   - S - Length of stroke in feet
   - N - Number of strokes per minute
   - T - Time expressed in minutes

   If a 3" diameter pump with a 7" stroke works at the rate of 30 strokes per minute, then, in one hour, this pump will deliver 4626.72 gallons.

   8.____

9. When exhaust steam from an industrial process is used for heating purposes, an extractor or separator should be used in order to catch and release air and water.

   9.____

10. The capacity rating of a steam trap selected should *always* be somewhat more than the actual amount of conden-sate to be handled.

    10.____

11. For efficient operation, each piece of equipment using steam should be trapped *individually* to insure positive circulation and proper air elimination.

    11.____

12. The height that a steam trap is capable of elevating condensate is dependent *only* on the amount of back pressure in the return.

    12.____

13. It is *important* that entrained air in the coils of unit heaters be quickly removed not only for quick heating and maximum efficiency but to get air out of the coil to prevent trouble due to corrosion. 13.____

14. Piping won't stand up and work efficiently without adequate support on strapping. Ample pipe hangers or supports on approximately 15-foot centers is considered *good* rule-of-thumb practice for the ordinary installation. 14.____

Questions 15-20.

DIRECTIONS: The figure on the next page shows some of piping and equipment mounted on or tied into a heating boiler. Questions 15 through 20, inclusive, relate to the piping and equipment shown in this sketch.

15. The letter A indicates breeching on which safety valves are *commonly* mounted. 15.____

16. The letter B shows location at which bottom blowdown is *usually* tied in. 16.____

17. The letter C indicates a symbol which represents a horizontal swing check valve. 17.____

18. The letter D shows the location at which make-up water is fed into the boiler. 18.____

19. The letter E shows the operating boiler water level. 19.____

20. The letter F points to a heat exchanger which is piped to take live steam from this boiler. 20.____

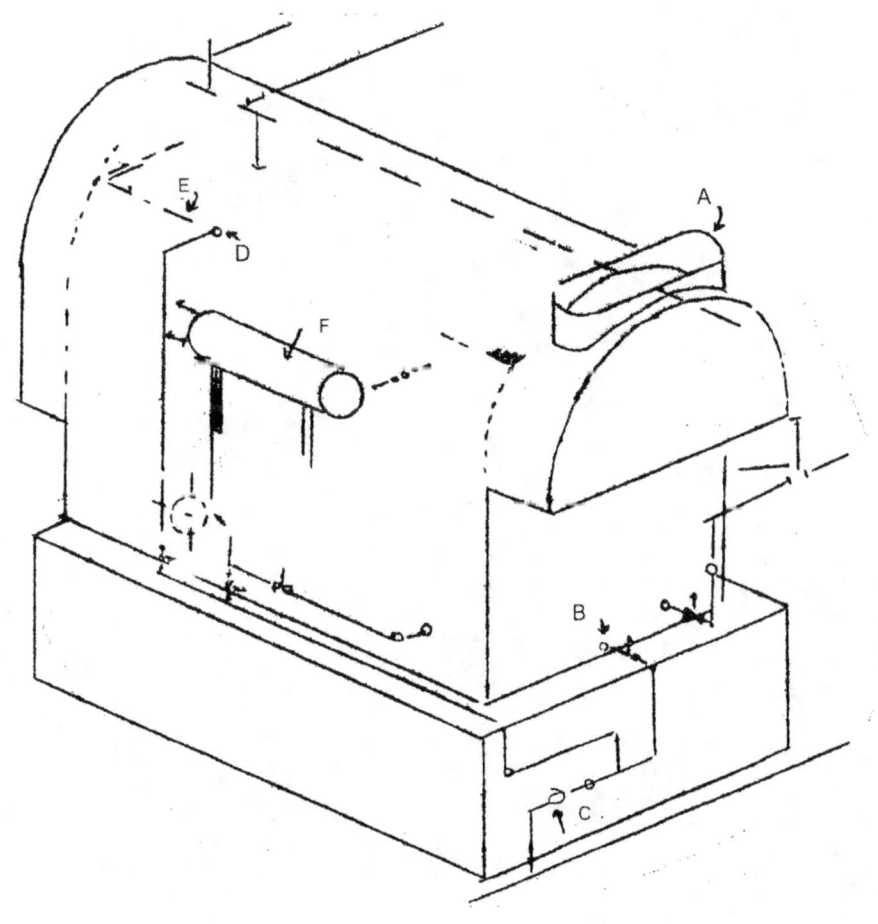

KEY (CORRECT ANSWERS)

1.	F		11.	T
2.	F		12.	F
3.	F		13.	T
4.	T		14.	F
5.	F		15.	F
6.	T		16.	T
7.	F		17.	F
8.	F		18.	F
9.	F		19.	T
10.	T		20.	F

EXAMINATION SECTION
TEST 1

DIRECTIONS: Each question or incomplete statement is followed by several suggested answers or completions. Select the one that BEST answers the question or completes the statement. *PRINT THE LETTER OF THE CORRECT ANSWER IN THE SPACE AT THE RIGHT.*

1. A steam heating boiler is classified as a low pressure boiler when it generates steam at a gage pressure of

    A. not more than 30 pounds per square inch
    B. not more than 25 pounds per square inch
    C. not more than 20 pounds per square inch
    D. 15 pounds per square inch or less

    1.____

2. A hot water heating boiler is classified as a low pressure boiler when it produces hot water at a gage pressure

    A. not more than 200 pounds per square inch
    B. not more than 175 pounds per square inch
    C. not more than 160 pounds per square inch
    D. equal to an absolute pressure of 200 pounds per square inch

    2.____

3. Of the following processes, the one which is NOT involved in the transfer of heat in a boiler from the hot gases to the water is

    A. radiation
    B. conduction
    C. convection
    D. evaporation

    3.____

4. The MINIMUM flue gas CO_2 reading permitted in a large metropolitan city is

    A. 5%   B. 8%   C. 12%   D. 16%

    4.____

5. The Ringelmann Chart is a device that is used for checking

    A. smoke density from a chimney
    B. boiler water condition
    C. percent CO_2 of the flue gas
    D. the carbon content of coal

    5.____

6. Low voltage control circuits for oil burners usually operate at a voltage of _____ volts.

    A. six (6)
    B. twelve (12)
    C. twenty-five (25)
    D. fifty (50)

    6.____

7. The connection known as a *Hartford Loop* is usually found on

    A. radiators
    B. high pressure hot water heaters
    C. low pressure unit heaters
    D. low pressure steam boilers

    7.____

8. Of the following types of fuel oils, the one that has the GREATEST heat value per gallon is _____ oil.

   A. diesel   B. #2   C. #4   D. #6

9. Of the following types of fuel, the one which has the HIGHEST heat content per pound (Btu/lb) is

   A. #2 fuel oil
   B. semibituminous coal
   C. semianthracite coal
   D. wood

10. The atomization of oil in the average domestic gun-type burner is accomplished by the

    A. air pressure
    B. pressure and centrifugal action of the oil
    C. low steam pressure
    D. draft effect of the stack

11. The type of fuel oil pump MOST commonly used with gun-type oil burners is the _____ type.

    A. centrifugal
    B. external or internal gear
    C. volute
    D. propeller

12. Chimney draft is usually measured in

    A. inches of mercury
    B. inches of water
    C. feet of water
    D. pounds per square inch

13. *Draft* that is produced over the fire or in a chimney without the use of any mechanical aids is generally known as _____ draft.

    A. balanced
    B. induced
    C. positive
    D. natural

14. Assume that a residential heating control system consists of a room thermostat, a limit control, a combustion control, a safety control, and a control relay. These controls would MOST likely be used with

    A. automatic gas-fired burners
    B. automatic oil-fired burners
    C. coal-fired stokers
    D. electric heating systems

15. A gauge that can be used for measuring either a vacuum or positive pressure in pounds per square inch is generally called a _____ gauge.

    A. compound
    B. pressure
    C. boiler
    D. vacuum

16. The purpose of a goose-neck connection to a Bourdon type steam gage is to

    A. prevent water getting into the gage tube
    B. prevent steam getting into the gage tube
    C. correct for trapped air in the line
    D. allow impurities to settle in the tube

17. The device that is generally used to reduce high pressure steam to low pressure steam is called a

    A. pressure relief valve
    B. pressure regulating valve
    C. condenser
    D. by-pass control valve

18. The MAXIMUM size of boiler safety valve that can be used on a low pressure boiler is

    A. 2"   B. $3\frac{1}{2}$"   C. $4\frac{1}{2}$"   D. $5\frac{1}{2}$"

19. If the water level in a steam heating boiler is unsteady, the probable cause may MOST likely be due to

    A. overfiring of boiler
    B. the use of a poor grade of fuel
    C. insufficient radiation in the heating system
    D. the use of an oversized boiler

20. The PRIMARY reason for using a gate valve in low pressure steam lines is to

    A. vary the steam pressure
    B. allow for quick opening
    C. reduce the flow of condensate to the boiler
    D. allow full free flow

21. Of the following types of valves, the one which is generally used to allow fluids to flow in one direction only is the

    A. gas cock   B. globe valve
    C. check valve   D. by-pass valve

22. The type of valve that is usually in a line with a swing check valve is a _____ valve.

    A. gate   B. diaphragm
    C. quick opening   D. globe

23. Excessive use of highly alkaline water in a boiler would probably result in boiler

    A. caustic embrittlement   B. priming
    C. foaming   D. corrosion

24. In a fire tube boiler, most of the soot usually accumulates

    A. on the inside surface of the tubes
    B. on the bridge wall
    C. in the combustion chamber
    D. on the outside surface of the tubes

25. Pneumatic tools are usually operated by

    A. steam   B. air   C. water   D. electricity

26. An *intercooler* is a device usually used in conjunction with a(n)

    A. boiler
    B. gear type oil pump
    C. centrifugal water pump
    D. air compressor

27. Of the following types of boilers, the one that is MOST commonly used for low pressure steam operation is the _____ boiler.

    A. Stirling
    B. cross-drum straight-tube
    C. cast iron vertical header logitudinal
    D. fire tube

28. The sum of the following pipe lengths, 15 5/8", 8 3/4", 30 5/6", and 20 1/2", is *most nearly*

    A. 77 1/8"   B. 76 3/16"   C. 75 3/16"   D. 74 5/16"

29. A boiler shell can sometimes be repaired temporarily by means of a

    A. soft patch and patch bolt
    B. hard patch and cap screws
    C. hard patch and rivets
    D. soft patch and rivets

30. The method generally used to provide rigidity for the internal flat surfaces of horizontal fire tube boilers is by

    A. riveting   B. staying   C. welding   D. caulking

31. The function of try-cocks on a boiler is PRIMARILY to

    A. drain the gage glass
    B. add water to the boiler
    C. check the gage glass reading
    D. blow down the water column

32. A boiler *blow-off* is usually connected

    A. to the steam compartment of the boiler
    B. next to the water column
    C. to the lowest water space available
    D. to the Hartford Loop

33. A boiler feedwater regulator automatically controls the

    A. water temperature in the boiler
    B. water pressure to the boiler
    C. feedwater treatment to the boiler
    D. water supply to the boiler

34. A feedwater heater in a steam generating plant is generally used to

    A. heat and condition water to the boiler
    B. provide make-up steam for the boiler
    C. feed hot water to plumbing fixtures
    D. increase feedwater pressure

35. If the outside diameter of a pipe is 6 inches and the wall thickness is $\frac{1}{2}$ inch, the inside area of this pipe, in square inches, is *most nearly*

   A. 15.7   B. 17.3   C. 19.6   D. 23.8

36. The type of pipe, used for water or gas, that should NOT be welded is _____ pipe.

   A. galvanized
   B. brass
   C. black wrought iron
   D. black steel

37. The instrument usually used to calibrate steam pressure gages is known as a _____ tester.

   A. lever-arm weight
   B. dead-weight
   C. Fyrite
   D. calibrated spring scale

38. A boiler horsepower is the evaporation from and at 212°F of _____ pounds of water per hour.

   A. 34.50   B. 30.50   C. 29.50   D. 25.50

39. A steam heating system that operates under both vacuum and low pressure conditions without use of a vacuum pump is known as a _____ system.

   A. forced return
   B. low pressure
   C. vacuum
   D. vapor

40. The purpose of an expansion tank in a hot water heating system is to

   A. add cold water to the system when needed
   B. prevent water hammer in the system
   C. allow for changes in the volume of water in the system
   D. store the water of the system when boiler is off the line

KEY (CORRECT ANSWERS)

1. D	11. B	21. C	31. C
2. C	12. B	22. A	32. C
3. D	13. D	23. A	33. D
4. B	14. B	24. A	34. A
5. A	15. A	25. B	35. C
6. C	16. B	26. D	36. A
7. D	17. B	27. D	37. B
8. D	18. C	28. C	38. A
9. A	19. A	29. A	39. D
10. B	20. D	30. B	40. C

TEST 2

DIRECTIONS: Each question or incomplete statement is followed by several suggested answers or completions. Select the one that BEST answers the question or completes the statement. *PRINT THE LETTER OF THE CORRECT ANSWER IN THE SPACE AT THE RIGHT.*

1. The pressure relief valve in a forced hot water heating system is generally mounted   1.____

    A. on top of the boiler
    B. on top of the air cushion tank
    C. in the hot water return line
    D. on the line between the circulating pump and the boiler

2. In a forced hot water circulating system, the circulating pump is usually controlled by a   2.____

    A. low-water cut out   B. room thermostat
    C. return-pump control   D. float

3. The diameter of a roof vent from an open expansion tank in a hot water heating system should be NOT less than   3.____

    A. 5"   B. 4"   C. 3"   D. 2"

4. If the circumference of a circle measures 12.566 inches, its diameter is equal to *most nearly*   4.____

    A. 2.75"   B. 3.00"   C. 3.50"   D. 4.00"

5. A valve that opens when its solenoid is energized and closes when the current is interrupted is known as a _____ valve.   5.____

    A. magnetic   B. thermostatic
    C. relay   D. shut-off

6. The device that shuts off the flow of fuel oil to a rotary cup type oil burner, in case of primary air failure, is generally known as a   6.____

    A. flame supervisor   B. pressuretrol
    C. aquastat   D. vaporstat

7. A device used to assure a proper temperature of No. 6 fuel oil before it is allowed to enter a burner is known as a   7.____

    A. thermostat   B. aquastat
    C. pyrostat   D. fustat

8. A device used to start the operation of line voltage equipment by means of a low voltage control circuit is called a   8.____

    A. circuit breaker   B. relay
    C. rectifier   D. variac

9. A pyrometer is generally used to measure the   9.____

    A. specific gravity of a liquid
    B. density of a gas

46

C. temperature of flue gas
D. percent of carbon dioxide

10. A low water cut-off on a boiler is usually operated by means of a   10._____

    A. bellows   B. helix   C. float   D. diaphragm

11. Assume that the water level in the gauge glass of a steaming boiler drops out of sight   11._____
    during a test of the low water cut-off.
    As an inspector, you

    A. order the boiler to be taken off the line
    B. assume the cut-off is working properly
    C. order more water to be put into the boiler
    D. order the drain valves to be opened immediately

12. The function of a *pressuretrol* on an oil-fired steam boiler is to keep the   12._____

    A. oil pressure constant
    B. steam pressure from exceeding a predetermined amount
    C. water pressure above 20 pounds per square inch
    D. draft pressure below atmosphere

13. A *remote control switch* for an oil burner should usually be located   13._____

    A. next to the three-way magnetic oil valve
    B. only at the boiler
    C. at the exit of the boiler room
    D. in the superintendent's office

14. A stack switch is a device that is used to shut off the oil burner in case of   14._____

    A. flame failure
    B. high steam pressure
    C. excessive flue gas temperature
    D. low water in boiler

15. A pressuretrol is usually connected directly to the   15._____

    A. water side of a boiler
    B. flue gas side of a boiler
    C. steam side of a boiler
    D. discharge side of fuel line

16. A modutrol motor on a typical automatic oil burner firing #6 oil may be used to directly   16._____
    control the

    A. speed of the oil pump or vaporstat
    B. primary air, secondary air, and oil control valve
    C. 3-way magnetic oil valve and magnetic gas valve
    D. electric fuel oil preheater and aquastat

Questions 17-20.

DIRECTIONS: Questions 17 to 20 inclusive are to be answered by referring to the drawing symbols of screwed fittings and valves shown below.

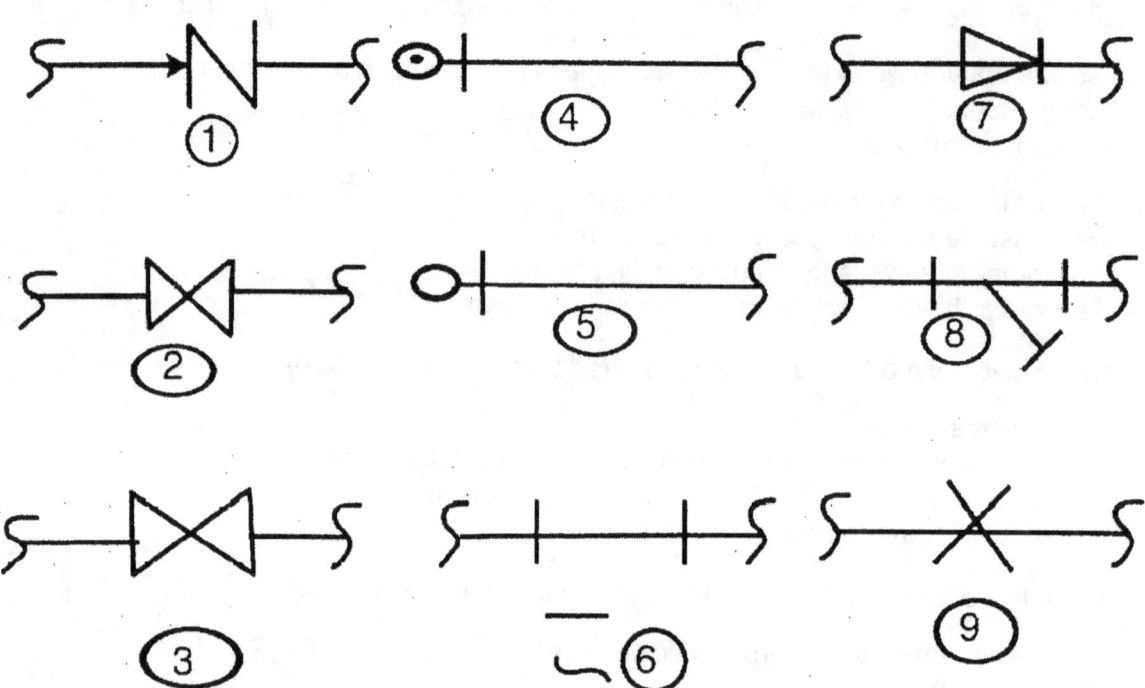

17. Referring to the above sketches, the one representing a turned-up elbow is numbered
    A. 4   B. 5   C. 6   D. 8

18. Referring to the above sketches, the one representing a check valve is numbered
    A. 1   B. 3   C. 7   D. 9

19. Referring to the above sketches, the one representing a globe valve is numbered
    A. 9   B. 3   C. 2   D. 1

20. Referring to the above sketches, the one representing a strainer is numbered
    A. 3   B. 7   C. 9   D. 8

21. The minimum size of pipe that should be used to connect a water column to a low pressure steam boiler is *most nearly*
    A. 3/8"   B. 1/2"   C. 3/4"   D. 1"

22. Of the following metals, the one which is classified as a ferrous metal is
    A. lead   B. iron   C. tin   D. zinc

23. Of the following types of pipe, the one which will expand the MOST when heated is
    A. copper   B. wrought iron
    C. steel   D. brass

4 (#2)

24. Of the following devices, the ones that are usually used to provide for expansion in a long horizontal run of hot water pipe are   24.____

    A. clamps   B. anchors
    C. swivel offsets   D. pipe stanchions

25. The MINIMUM diameter of pipe that may be used for gas piping is   25.____

    A. 3/4"   B. 5/8"   C. 1/2"   D. 3/8"

26. The type of thread that is used on standard iron pipe size brass pipe is known as the   26.____

    A. Witworth Standard   B. Briggs Standard
    C. British Association   D. Standard Acme

27. The taper on a standard pipe thread is *most nearly* _____ to the foot.   27.____

    A. 1/8"   B. 1/4"   C. 1/2"   D. 3/4"

28. Of the following statements concerning the use of lamp wick on screwed pipe joints, the one which is *most nearly* CORRECT is that   28.____

    A. it may suggest the existence of imperfect threads
    B. it is the best modern day practice
    C. the joints are strengthened
    D. pipe compound is not needed

29. Of the following wrenches, the one which is used MOST often for making up connections to a boiler is the _____ wrench.   29.____

    A. monkey   B. open end   C. strap   D. pipe

30. Boiler fusible plugs are usually filled with   30.____

    A. lead   B. copper   C. tin   D. solder

31. The capacity, in gallons, of a 10'-0" diameter by 21'-0" high cylindrical tank with flat heads is *most nearly*   31.____

    A. 1650   B. 2100   C. 6900   D. 12,500

32. "The water level in the gage glass was *dormant* during the peak load conditions." As used in this sentence, the word *dormant* means *most nearly*   32.____

    A. fluctuating   B. inactive
    C. clean   D. foaming

33. The instructor's words were understood but *irrelevant*. As used in this sentence, the word *irrelevant* means *most nearly*   33.____

    A. unchallenging to the audience
    B. unconvincing to the audience
    C. not bearing upon the subject under discussion
    D. not based upon facts

34. The MOST important requirement of a good inspectional report is that it should be   34.____

    A. properly addressed   B. lengthy
    C. clear and brief   D. spelled correctly

35. Building superintendents frequently inquire about departmental inspectional procedures. Of the following, it is BEST to

    A. advise them to write to the department for an official reply
    B. refuse as the inspectional procedure is a restricted matter
    C. briefly explain the procedure to them
    D. avoid the inquiry by changing the subject

36. In making an inspection of a boiler repair job in progress in a private building, an inspector's PRIMARY concern should be to

    A. avoid conversation with the building superintendent
    B. concentrate on the workmanship of the men
    C. anticipate construction problems before they occur
    D. ascertain whether or not the repair job is in accordance with the code and regulations of the department

Questions 37-40.

DIRECTIONS: Questions 37 to 40, inclusive, are to be answered in accordance with the following paragraph.

A low pressure hot water boiler shall include a relief valve or valves of a capacity such that with the heat generating equipment operating at maximum, the pressure cannot rise more than 20 percent above the maximum allowable working pressure (set pressure) if that is 30 p.s.i. gage or less, nor more than 10 percent if it is more than 30 p.s.i. gage. The difference between the set pressure and the pressure at which the valve is relieving is known as "overpressure or accumulation." If the steam relieving capacity in pounds per hour is calculated, it shall be determined by dividing by 1,000 the maximum Btu output at the boiler nozzle obtainable from the heat generating equipment, or by multiplying the square feet of heating surface by five.

37. In accordance with the above paragraph, the capacity of a relief valve should be computed on the basis of

    A. size of boiler
    B. maximum rated capacity of generating equipment
    C. average output of the generating equipment
    D. minimum capacity of generating equipment

38. In accordance with the above paragraph, with a set pressure of 30 p.s.i. gage, the overpressure should NOT be more than _____ p.s.i.

    A. 3   B. 6   C. 33   D. 36

39. In accordance with the above paragraph, a relief valve should start relieving at a pressure equal to the _____ pressure.

    A. set
    B. over
    C. overpressure minus set
    D. set pressure plus over

40. In accordance with the above paragraph, the steam relieving capacity can be computed by

    A. multiplying the maximum BTU output by 5
    B. dividing the pounds of steam per hour by 1000
    C. dividing the maximum BTU output by the square feet of heating surface
    D. dividing the maximum BTU output by 1000

40._____

KEY (CORRECT ANSWERS)

1. A	11. A	21. D	31. D
2. B	12. B	22. B	32. B
3. B	13. C	23. A	33. C
4. D	14. A	24. C	34. C
5. A	15. C	25. D	35. C
6. D	16. B	26. B	36. D
7. B	17. A	27. D	37. B
8. B	18. A	28. A	38. B
9. C	19. B	29. D	39. D
10. C	20. D	30. C	40. D

52

EXAMINATION SECTION
TEST 1

DIRECTIONS: Each question or incomplete statement is followed by several suggested answers or completions. Select theone that BEST answers the question or completes statement. *PRINT THE LETTER OF THE CORRECT ANSWER IN THE SPACE AT THE RIGHT.*

1. Difficulties likely to be encountered in operating a water tube boiler are: 1.____
    I. Foaming and priming,scale formation or oil deposits on the heating surfaces and caustic embrittlement
    II. Leaking baffles; slag and soot formation on the tubes
    III. Excessive leakage of air through the setting
    IV. Inadequate steam control
   The CORRECT answer is:

   A. I, II only   B. I, II, III   C. I, II, IV   D. II, III, IV

2. A boiler suitable for *high* ratings must 2.____
    I. have good water circulation
    II. produce dry steam
    III. not be subject to excessive variation in water level when the rating changes
    IV. produce wet steam
   The CORRECT answer is:

   A. I, II, III   B. I, III, IV   C. I, II only   D. II, III only

3. The principal losses which vary with the boiler rating are 3.____

   A. dry gas loss and combustible in refuse
   B. undeveloped heat in the form of carbon monoxide and other combustible gases
   C. radiation losses
   D. all of the above

4. When dirty steam is admitted to a steam turbine, it is *likely* to 4.____
    I. plug up the nozzles
    II. settle into the bottom of the fixed blades
    III. form deposits on the blades
    IV. cause excessive erosion of the nozzles and the
   The CORECT answer is:

   A. I, II only   B. II, IV only   C. I, II, III   D. I, II, III, IV

5. High water level or wide fluctuations in water level due to improper feedwater regulation or fluctuating load is *likely* to give 5.____

   A. high rates of evaporation
   B. a higher surface tension of the boiler water
   C. wet steam
   D. all of the above

6. Convection type superheaters are located

   A. between the passes of generating tubes
   B. near the furnace
   C. in the breeching
   D. in the furnace wall

7. Under the conditions in which anaaccumulation test is run, the safety valve equipment should be sufficient to prevent an excess pressure of no more than _____ percent above the maximum allowable working preassure.

   A. 50   B. 30   C. 20   D. 7

8. The FIRST to blow should be

   A. either the superheater or steam drum safety valve
   B. the superheater
   C. the steam drum safety valve
   D. both; they must blow at the same time

9. When a thin gauge boiler tube is *overexpanded*

   A. the tube is weakened and seat leakage may result
   B. its thickness at the seat is reduced, with no ill effects, however
   C. the seats become enlarged
   D. the boiler will explode

10. Welded joints of boiler drums are
    I. not as strong as riveted joints
    II. equally as strong as riveted joints
    III. as strong as the solid plate
    IV. can be stronger than the solid plate
    The CORRECT answer is :

    A. I, II   B. II, III   C. III, IV   D. I, IV

11. Economizers are MOST effective when constructed accoeding to the _____ flow principle.

    A. counter   B. straight   C. reverse   D. current

12. Advantage gained by the use of aie preheaters are

    A. improved efficiency by reclaining heat from the flue gases with an accelerated and improved combustion
    B. increased boiler capacity with a low-fixed charge making it possible to utilize a cheaper grade of coal
    C. high efficiency over a wide range of rating
    D. all of the above

13. The *proper* mixture of air and coal dust is

    A. difficult to obtain   B. too rich to explode
    C. highly explosive   D. non-flamable

14. In purchasing a water tube boiler for high ratings, which type of tube should be selected?   14._____

    A. Narrow type
    B. Wide type
    C. Either type depending upon the fuel used
    D. It makes no difference

15. When there is NO water mist in the steam, only water vapor, at a temprature corresponding to the preassure, then the steam is termed   15._____

    A. dry saturated   B. wet
    C. superheated   D. over inflated

16. When the moisture content of steam is either too high or too low to be accurately determined by a throttling calorimeter, you should   16._____

    A. change the orifice of the throttling calorimeter
    B. insulate the calorimeter to prevent rediation loss
    C. use a seperating calorimeter
    D. all of the above

17. Which of the following may be used for providing for expansion in steam lines?   17._____

    A. Long radius and U-bends
    B. Double-swing screwed joints
    C. Expansion joints
    D. All of the above

18. Which *valve* should be installed on the steam header to prevent the other boilers from feeding steam back into a boiler which has failed because of battery failure?   18._____

    A. check   B. steam header
    C. non-return   D. expansion

19. The advantage of a closed feedwater heater are that   19._____

    A. the contamination in the steam is not transferred to the condensate
    B. the water is forced throuh the heater, with one pump utilized to force the water through several heaters
    C. these heaters prevent the contamination of the water with with oxygen
    D. all of the above

20. A boiler is said to be in the package-boiler field if the evaporation is _____ lb. of steam per hour.   20._____

    A. 1,000 to 200,000   B. 200,000 to 300,000
    C. 300,000 to 500,000   D. 500,000 to 1,000,000

21. Combustion control is IMPORTANT because of   21._____

    A. increasing price of fuel and materials
    B. projected shortages of fossil fuels
    C. increasing cost of labor
    D. all of the above

22. In order to maintain the HIGHEST combustion efficiency, consistent with economical operation, the

    A. fuel must have a high Btu value
    B. combustion air must be preheated
    C. air and fuel must be proportioned
    D. all of the above

23. Advantages derived from automatic combustion control are

    A. savings in fuel
    B. increased capacity
    C. continuous operation with safety
    D. all of the above

24. The CORRECT percentage of excess air is

    A. 10 pounds of air per pound of fuel
    B. the air required to burn the fuel
    C. that which will keep to a minimum the total losses due to excess air and unburned fuel
    D. all of the above

25. The master Air Pilot Valve of the pneumatic combustion control system can be actuated by a

    A. Bourdon tube   B. capillary tube
    C. thermobulb   D. flame

26. Daily maintenance of a pneumatic combustion control system should consist of

    A. inspecting air cleaners and replacing the filtering medium if necessary
    B. cleaning gears and oil mechanisms
    C. blowing out air lines on air flow
    D. all of the above

27. The CHIEF problem in the use of combustion control equipment is

    A. to purchase one that is easy to operate and maintain
    B. to select one that can properly distribute the load
    C. the selection of the proper combination and arrangement of elements to suit the operating characteristics of the plant
    D. all of the above

28. MOST combustions controls have
    I. the iddividual boiler control panel receive the impulse and transmit it to a draft regulator and a fuel air ratio delay
    II. a preassure helix or Bourdon tube
    III: a beam movement, transmitted through suitable linkage
    IV. a movable magnet bar which makes contact in a mercury switch
    The CORRECT answer is:

    A. I, II   B. I, III   C. II, III   D. III, IV

29. The MAIN set point in a master control refers to steam 29._____
    I. temperature
    II. flow
    III. pressure
    IV. humidity
    The CORRECT answer is:

    A. I, III   B. II, III   C. II, IV   D. III, IV

30. The most important control in a steam generating plant is the 30._____

    A. damper regulator   B. fuel air ratio control
    C. fuel ahut off control   D. none of the above

31. The major elements controlled by a good combustion control system are: 31._____
    I. Steam preassure
    II. Air vlume
    III. Fuel feed
    IV. Furnace draft
    The CORRECT answer is:

    A. I, II, III   B. II, III, IV
    C. I, II, IV   D. I, II, III, IV

32. The *primary* unit of MOST combustion control system is the _____ control. 32._____

    A. air flow   B. fuel feed
    C. master steam preassure   D. furnace draft

33. Combustion control can 33._____

    A. automatically control furnace draft
    B. adjust the boiler output to load demands
    C. maintain the proper fuel and air ratio
    D. all of the above

34. Which of the statements below is *least likely* to be true of modern combustion control equipment? 34._____

    A. The operator relieved of the work of making minor ad-justments, will be free to attend to more important duties in the operation of the boiler room
    B. The operator relieved of the vaiious phases of routine operation can now be removed from the payroll because he is no longer needed for plant operations
    C. Combustion control is a natural development of the perfection of instruments with the operator's job becoming more technical, and therefore additional education and training in technology is required
    D. All of the above

35. When changes occur in the heating value of fuel, i.e., moisture content, etc., a change must be made in the 35._____

    A. furnace draft   B. fuel-air ratio
    C. steam pressure   D. all of the above

36. Steam turbines can be ruined because of 36.____
    A. slug of water
    B. vibration
    C. overspeed trip not working
    D. all of the above

37. If a strainer was removed from the steam line to a turbine 37.____
    A. scale would foul the emergency-throttle valve
    B. dissolve solids would go into the turbine
    C. the steam will reach the blades with greater force
    D. all of the above

38. Turbine casting can explode because of 38.____
    A. high pressure   B. high speeds
    C. a closed exaust valve   D. all of the above

39. The PRINCIPAL concern in turbine operation are to 39.____
    A. avoid vibrations
    B. preserve a perfect state of balance
    C. prevent overheating strains
    D. all of the above

40. The spindle will be HOTTER with *only* the seal steam on 40.____
    A. while the turbine is in operation
    B. while the turbine is NOT in operation
    C. in the packing space *only*
    D. all of the above

KEY (CORRECT ANSWERS)

1.	B	11.	A	21.	D	31.	D
2.	A	12.	D	22.	C	32.	C
3.	D	13.	C	23.	D	33.	D
4.	D	14.	C	24.	C	34.	B
5.	C	15.	A	25.	A	35.	B
6.	A	16.	C	26.	D	36.	D
7.	D	17.	D	27.	C	37.	A
8.	B	18.	C	28.	A	38.	D
9.	A	19.	D	29.	A	39.	D
10.	C	20.	A	30.	D	40.	C

TEST 2

DIRECTIONS: Each question or incomplete statement is followed by several suggested answers or completions. Select the one that BEST answers the question or completes the statement. *PRINT THE LETTER OF THE CORRECT ANSWER IN THE SPACE AT THE RIGHT.*

1. If a turbine has been stopped and allowed to cool for a short time and then started *too quietly*, it is possible that the

    A. wheels and dummies can become distorted
    B. casing will become damaged
    C. oil will flood the bearings
    D. all of the above

    1.____

2. What device below is used for overspeed?
    I. An Inertia governor
    II. A gravity governor
    III. Combined throttle
    IV. Emergency stop valve

    The CORRECT answer is:

    A. I, II, III   B. II, III, IV
    C. I, III, IV   D. I, II, IV

    2.____

3. How much steam should be admitted to the valve chest?

    A. Give it very little steam by merely cracking the throttle
    B. Open the throttle all the way
    C. Admit sufficient steam to give trubine immediately action without filling the different stages, causing heating of the upper half of the casing
    D. All of the above

    3.____

4. A sluggish governor can be caused by
    I. the spring being too tense
    II. the steam is not hot enough
    III. circulating oil too cold
    IV. steam being too hot

    The CORRECT answer is:

    A. I, III   B. I, IV   C. II, III   D. II, IV

    4.____

5. A turbine has been operating successfully without any signs of trouble.
   Then, all of a sudden, the shaft or spindle begins to sway from end to end and the roller-thrust has let go.
   What must the engineer do to bring the machine to a stop *without* damage?

    A. Close the throttle Immediately
    B. Let it go, the overspeed governor will take over
    C. Keep a strong field on the generator until practically the last turn of the shaft
    D. All of the above

    5.____

6. A unit of the extraction type spilled into a common tenpound line with several auxiliaries such as small steam engines, turbines,and reducing valves.
What danger will be present ?

   A. The non-return valve on the extraction line will "hang up" and allow ten pound steam to enter the turbine
   B. The non-return valve on the extraction line will "hang up"and allow high pressure steam to enter the ten lb.line
   C. No danger is involved
   D. All of the above

7. A steam turbine operating a generator of ,1000 K.W. or more

   A. adequate day to day inspection
   B. anual inspection with all of the covers removed
   C. monthly inspection for minor defects,leaks and governor wear
   D. all of the above

8. If an inspection reveals that it is necessary to rebucket a stage or more,the spindle can be
   I. left in the bearings
   II. removed and placed on horses
   III. raised by a crane and rebucketed while being suspended in he slings
   IV. cut

   The CORRECT answer is:

   A. I, II   B. I, III   C. II, III   D. III, IV

9. What replacements could the governor *reasonably* be expected to require during an overhaul?

   A. pins   B. Linkage
   C. Knife-edges   D. All of the above

10. As the coupling is butted together, the thickness at point of a sheet of tissue paper can

    A. make little difference
    B. prevent the companion from matching
    C. throw the outboard rr generator end bearings out several thousands of an inch
    D. all of the above

11. For all designs of single row impllse blading, MAXIMUM efficiency of the turbine is reached when the speed of the turbine is so adjusted that the speed of the blades is _____ the speed of the steam entering the blades.

    A. one-fourth   B. one-half
    C. equal to   D. twice

12. A method used to reduce the blade speed by absorbing the kinetic energy of a jet in more than one row ofmoving blades in a single preassure stage is called _____ staging.

    A. tandem   B. multiple   C. velocity   D. duplex

13. A two-stage machine used to operate at the *same efficiency* of a single blade machine MUST rotate at _____ the speed.

    A. twice B. equal to C. one-half D. one quarter

14. Since any wear of the main (radial) bearings will cause the shaft and rotor to drop relative to the casing, with consequentat misalignment at all times must be taken to determine the condition of the

    A. blades B. shaft C. bearings D. rotor

15. The component, $V \sin \alpha$, exerts a force parallel to the axis of the rotor. This α, at some speeds, is cared for by blade design.
    But, in general, a residual axial thrust must be compensated by

    A. thrust bearing B. coupling
    C. variable stresses D. rotating

16. Steam is classified with respect to pressure as

    A. atmospheric B. low pressure
    C. high pressure D. all of the above

17. A calorimeter is an instrument used to

    A. measure dry steam
    B. define steam
    C. determine the quality of steam
    D. measure heat

18. What condition below favors SUPERHEATED steam?

    A. High degree of expansion of steam
    B. Slow speed of engine
    C. Constant load
    D. All of the above

19. If a turbine has a sudden increase of lube-oil pressure, what would NOT be the major problem?

    A. Clogged oil line
    B. Too much back pressure on the bearing
    C. Dirty strainer
    D. Too much oil in the system

20. The main bearing on a turbine is lubricated by

    A. a hand oil can B. the splash system
    C. the force-feed method D. greasing the bearing

21. An advantage of a turbine over a reciprocating engine is that it

    A. better utilizes a high vacuum
    B. permits higher temperatures and preassures
    C. eliminates vibrating reciprocating parts
    D. has an extreme overload capacity

22. Some lifting injector types are :
    I. Double tube
    II. Single tube
    III. vacuum tube
    IV. Condenser
    The CORRECT answer is:

    A. I, III   B. I, II   C. II, III   D. I, IV

23. An evaporator regulator depends upon the
    I. proportion on the inner tube filled with steam
    II. water level in the boiler
    III. steam in the inner tube which will evaporate the water in the enclosed vessel
    IV. evaporation in order to supply pressure on the feed diaphragm, hereby opening the valve to some point corresponding to the amount of water evaporated
    The CORRECT answer is:

    A. I, II   B. II, III   C. I, II, IV   D. I, II, III, IV

24. An injector is used for forcing
    A. oil into a boiler
    B. water into the boiler
    C. steam into an oil pre-heater
    D. water into a surface condenser

25. Important parts of an injector are the
    I. steam nozzle
    II. combining tube
    III. exhaust tube
    IV. water inlet and overflow
    The CORRECT answer is:

    A. I, II   B. II, III   C. II, III, IV   D. I, II, III, IV

26. Types of injectors are
    I. Automatic
    II. Lifting or non-lifting
    III. Adjustable nozzle
    IV. Exhaust and positive
    The CORRECT answer is:

    A. I, II, III   B. II, III, IV   C. I, II, IV   D. I, II, III, IV

27. What is the purpose of steam trap?
    I. A steam trap is an automatic device which allows the passage of water also prevents the escaping of steam before the steam is condensed
    II. To drain the condensate from the steam lines
    III. To re-route the steam back to the condensate pump
    IV. To drain the impurities from condensate line
    The CORRECT answer is:

    A. I, II   B. II, III   C. II, IV   D. I, IV

28. Types of trap are:
    I. Float and thermostatic
    II. Below
    III. Bucket
    IV. Impulse

    The CORRECT answer is:

    A. I, II
    B. II, III, IV
    C. I, III, IV
    D. I, II, III, IV

29. You can detect if a trap is blowing by

    A. removing the trap from the line and replacing it
    B. isolating the trap, and opening it for inspection
    C. checking the strainer
    D. checking the temprature on both sides of the trap; if the temprature is the same on both sides, then the trap is blowing steam through

30. A high pressure drip trap is one that

    A. drips high ressure steam
    B. is attached to a high pressure steam line and returns to the boiler
    C. is connected on the bottom of a high pressure steam line,
    D. and dumps the high pressure condensate into a lowpressure line
    E. is attached to a high pressure steam line trapping all the high pressure condensate at the end of the main

31. A trap Is installed on a condensate line by

    A. hooking up with a valve before the trap
    B. installing with a strainer after the trap, with a valve between
    C. installing the trap with a strainer before the trap, and a valve after
    D. installing a valve on the line from the unit, then installing a strainer, union, trap, another union, and a valve

32. Which of the following is(are) IMPORTANT part(s) of a loop?
    I. Riser
    II. Goose neck
    III. Condenser
    IV. Drop leg

    The CORRECT answer is:

    A. I, III, IV
    B. II, III, I
    C. II, III, IV
    D. I, II, III, IV

33. A separator is used for separating
    I. water from oil
    II. moisture from steam
    III. oxygen from water
    IV. oil from gas

    The CORRECT answer is:

    A. I, II
    B. II, III
    C. I, II, IV
    D. I, II, III, IV

34. A separator is *normally* placed as close to a(n)
    I. engine as possible to avoid condensate from entering the engine
    II. boiler as possible
    III. receiver tank as possible
    IV. all of the above
    The CORRECT answer is:

    A. I, II, III
    B. II, III, IV
    C. I, III, IV
    D. I, II, III, IV

35. Separation of moisture is caused by

    A. high steam temperature
    B. sufficient vacuum
    C. centrifugal force, or gravity as a secondary force
    D. a steam loop

36. A _____ is *usually* attached to a separator.

    A. gauge glass
    B. drain cock
    C. reservoir
    D. all of the above

37. A DRY PIPE is used for

    A. an internal separator in the steam drum to separate the moisture from the steam before the steam enters the main steam line
    B. separating moisture from compressed air
    C. removing oil from water
    D. removing impurities from feedwater

38. The _____ valve supplies water to a boiler.

    A. throttle   B. globe   C. regulator   D. pilot

39. Some type of feedwater regulator are the
    I. buoyancy float
    II. thermostatic
    III. specific gravity
    IV. diaphragm
    The CORRECT answer is:

    A. I, II, III
    B. II, III, IV
    C. I, II, IV
    D. I, II, III, IV

40. An expansion regulator depends on
    I. a thermostatic tube
    II. a lever and a feedwater valve
    III. equalizing pipes connected to the steam and water space of the boiler
    IV. a feedwater pump with a governor
    The CORRECT answer is:

    A. I, II, III
    B. II, III, IV
    C. I, III, IV
    D. I, II, III, IV

KEY (CORRECT ANSWERS)

1. A	11. B	21. D	31. D
2. C	12. C	22. B	32. D
3. A	13. C	23. D	33. D
4. A	14. C	24. B	34. D
5. C	15. A	25. D	35. C
6. A	16. D	26. D	36. D
7. D	17. C	27. A	37. A
8. A	18. D	28. D	38. C
9. D	19. B	29. D	39. D
10. C	20. C	30. C	40. D

EXAMINATION SECTION
TEST 1

DIRECTIONS: Each question or incomplete statement is followed by several suggested answers or completions. Select the one that BEST answers the question or completes the statement. *PRINT THE LETTER OF THE CORRECT ANSWER IN THE SPACE AT THE RIGHT.*

1. In high pressure electric generating plants in large buildings, heating the feedwater from 70° F to 180° F with exhaust steam usually will DECREASE the fuel consumption by   1.____

   A. 5%   B. 10%   C. 15%   D. 20%

2. The direct room radiator with a pneumatically controlled steam heating system is cold, while the adjoining rooms are heated adequately.   2.____
   Of the following, the FIRST thing you would check in the room is the

   A. steam pipe in the room before the pneumatic steam valve
   B. thermostat
   C. pneumatic steam valve
   D. thermostatic trap

3. The USUAL vacuum gage on a steam heating system reads in   3.____

   A. inches of vacuum   B. feet of mercury
   C. inches of water   D. feet of water

4. In a mechanical pressure type burner using #6 oil heated to 230° F by steam, the oil is atomized by   4.____

   A. centrifugal force   B. steam temperature
   C. oil temperature   D. oil pressure

5. A vaporstat with separate motor driven oil pump used on a fully automatic heavy oil burning rotary cup installation is GENERALLY used to   5.____

   A. keep the boiler pressure within proper limits
   B. regulate the pressure of the primary air
   C. regulate the pressure of the secondary air
   D. shut down the burner when primary air failure occurs

6. In estimating the amount of work being done by a steam driven water pump, the one of the following items which is usually the MOST important in the calculation of pump horsepower is the   6.____

   A. temperature of the water
   B. suction lift
   C. steam pressure
   D. gallons pumped

7. The term *fixture unit* USUALLY refers to   7.____

   A. the number of lamp sockets in an electric lighting fixture
   B. the number of fixtures in a room or building

67

C. a rate of flow
D. amperes per second

8. In a hot water heating system, it may be necessary to *bleed* radiators to

    A. relieve high steam pressure
    B. permit entrapped air to escape
    C. allow condensate to return to the boiler
    D. drain off waste water

9. Which oil would have the GREATEST sulphur content?

    A. #2　　　B. #6　　　C. #1　　　D. #4

10. A *scrubber* would be MOST commonly found on a

    A. vacuum pump
    B. snow plow
    C. incinerator
    D. auditorium fresh air blower

11. Combustion efficiency can be determined from an appropriate chart used in conjunction with

    A. steam temperature and steam pressure
    B. flue gas temperature and percentage of CO_2
    C. flue gas temperature and fuel heating value
    D. oil temperature and steam pressure

12. One of the possible results of closing ashpit doors to regulate draft is

    A. warping or melting of grates
    B. reduced formation of clinkers
    C. steam will become superheated
    D. live coals will fall into the ashpit

13. The MOST important reason for blowing down a boiler water column and gauge glass is to

    A. prevent the gauge glass level from rising too high
    B. relieve stresses in the gauge glass
    C. insure a true water level reading
    D. insure a true pressure gauge reading

14. The secondary voltage of a transformer used for ignition in a fuel oil burner has a range of MOST NEARLY _____ volts.

    A. 120 to 240　　　　　B. 440 to 660
    C. 660 to 1,200　　　　D. 5,000 to 15,000

15. Assume that during the month of April there were 3 days with an average outdoor temperature of 30° F, 7 days with 40° F, 10 days with 50° F, 3 days with 60° F, and 7 days with 65°F. The number of degree days for the month was

    A. 330　　　B. 445　　　C. 595　　　D. 1,150

16. The pH of boiler feedwater is USUALLY maintained within the range of

    A. 4 to 5   B. 6 to 7   C. 10 to 12   D. 13 to 14

17. The admission of steam to the coils of a domestic hot water supply tank is regulated by a(n)

    A. pressure regulating valve
    B. immersion type temperature gauge
    C. check valve
    D. thermostatic control valve

18. The device which senses primary air failure in a rotary cup oil burner is USUALLY called a(n)

    A. vaporstat   B. anemometer
    C. venturi   D. pressure gauge

19. A vacuum pump is used in a(n) _____ heating system.

    A. steam   B. hot air   C. hot water   D. electric

20. An expansion tank is used in a(n) _____ heating system.

    A. steam   B. hot air   C. hot water   D. electric

21. The thermostat in the office area of a public building should have a winter daytime setting of about _____ °F.

    A. 50   B. 60   C. 70   D. 80

22. A lazy bar is MOST often associated with

    A. radiators   B. vents   C. fences   D. boilers

23. The domestic hot water in a large public building is circulated by

    A. gravity flow
    B. a pump which runs continuously
    C. a pump which is controlled by water pressure
    D. a pump which is controlled by water temperature

24. Of the following, the hacksaw blade BEST suited for cutting thin-walled tubing is one which has _____ teeth/inch.

    A. 14   B. 18   C. 24   D. 32

25. The emergency switch for a fully automatic oil burner is USUALLY located

    A. at the entrance to the boiler room
    B. on the burner
    C. at the electrical distribution panel in the boiler room
    D. at the electric service meter panel

KEY (CORRECT ANSWERS)

1. B
2. A
3. A
4. D
5. D
6. D
7. C
8. B
9. B
10. C

11. B
12. A
13. C
14. D
15. B
16. C
17. D
18. A
19. A
20. C

21. C
22. D
23. D
24. D
25. A

TEST 2

DIRECTIONS: Each question or incomplete statement is followed by several suggested answers or completions. Select the one that BEST answers the question or completes the statement. *PRINT THE LETTER OF THE CORRECT ANSWER IN THE SPACE AT THE RIGHT.*

1. A compound gauge is calibrated to read 1.____

   A. pressure *only*
   B. vacuum *only*
   C. vacuum and pressure
   D. temperature and humidity

2. In a mechanical pressure-atomizing type oil burner, the oil is atomized by using an atomizing tip and 2.____

   A. steam pressure
   B. pump pressure
   C. compressed air
   D. a spinning cup

3. A good over-the-fire draft in a natural draft furnace should be APPROXIMATELY _____ inches of water _____ . 3.____

   A. 5.0; positive pressure
   B. 0.05; positive pressure
   C. 0.05; vacuum
   D. 5.0; vacuum

4. When it is necessary to add chemicals to a heating boiler, it should be done 4.____

   A. immediately after boiler blowdown
   B. after the boiler has been cleaned internally of sludge, scale, and other foreign matter
   C. at periods when condensate flow to the boiler is small
   D. at a time when there is a heavy flow of condensate to the boiler

5. The modutrol motor on a rotary cup oil burner burning #6 fuel oil automatically operates the primary air damper, 5.____

   A. secondary air damper, and oil metering valve
   B. secondary air damper, and magnetic oil valve
   C. oil metering valve, a'nd magnetic oil valve
   D. and magnetic oil valve

6. The manual-reset pressuretrol is classified as a _____ control. 6.____

   A. safety and operating
   B. limit and operating
   C. limit and safety
   D. limit, operating, and safety

7. If you had too much oil, what would you do for good combustion? 7.____

   A. Increase secondary air
   B. Increase primary air
   C. Increase both
   D. Lower oil pressure

8. *Cascading* of raw city water when filling a cleaned boiler should be avoided because it 8.____

   A. is harmful to the mud drum
   B. adds additional free oxygen in the boiler

C. adds considerable time to the filling procedure
D. will stress tube and sheet joints

9. The average temperature on a day in January was 24°F. The number of degree days for that day was

    A. 12   B. 24   C. 41   D. 48

10. With the same outdoor winter temperatures, the load on a heating boiler starting up is greater than the normal morning load MAINLY because of

    A. loss of heat escaping through the stack
    B. steam required to heat boiler water and piping to radiators
    C. viscosity of the fuel oil
    D. low outdoor temperatures

11. The FIRST operation when starting a boiler after it has been on bank overnight should be to

    A. blow down the boiler
    B. clean the furnace
    C. check the gate valves
    D. look at the water gauge and try the gauge cocks

12. Proper combustion of fuel is obtained when

    A. the flue gases contain a large percentage of carbon monoxide
    B. black smoke appears in the flue gases
    C. there is 10 to 15 percent carbon dioxide in the flue gases
    D. the flame of the fire is high enough to reach the fire tubes

13. The vertical pipes leading from the steam mains to the radiators are called

    A. expansion joints   B. radiant coils
    C. drip lines   D. risers

14. Try cocks are used to

    A. determine the exact water level in the boiler
    B. find the approximate water level in the boiler
    C. learn if steam is being generated in the boiler
    D. obtain an approximate idea of the steam pressure

15. If a ton of anthracite coal occupies approximately 40 cubic feet, the space required, in cubic yards, for 135 tons of coal is

    A. 200   B. 128.6   C. 600   D. 40

16. During the winter heating season, it is BEST practice to blow down the boiler

    A. once a month
    B. twice daily
    C. only when new grates are installed
    D. once a day

17. A boiler blow-off valve is PRIMARILY used to 17.____

    A. maintain constant boiler pressure
    B. drain water from the boiler
    C. allow air to enter boiler when proper temperature is reached
    D. reduce boiler pressure

18. When a room becomes heated above the upper temperature setting of a thermostat 18.____
    which controls a check damper, the damper is

    A. automatically closed to reduce the air supply
    B. opened to admit more air
    C. not affected, but the supply of the boiler is increased
    D. partially closed and the water supply of the boiler is increased

19. The device which protects the boiler from damage due to low water is the 19.____

    A. fusible plug   B. fusible link
    C. vaporstat   D. aquastat

20. In a low-pressure fire-tube boiler, the oil burner should be shut off BEFORE 20.____

    A. operating the soot blower
    B. taking a flue gas sample
    C. blowing down the boiler
    D. blowing down the water column

21. A domestic hot water circulating pump is started and stopped automatically by means of 21.____
    a(n) _____ line.

    A. pressuretrol in the supply
    B. pressuretrol in the return
    C. aquastat in the supply
    D. aquastat in the return

22. On a steam-heated domestic hot water generator, the device which acts to PREVENT 22.____
    damage to the coils due to a high internal pressure differential between the coil and the
    tank is the

    A. pressure relief valve   B. vacuum breaker
    C. air vent valve   D. steam trap

23. In the city, the rules and regulations concerning the cleaning of a water tank which is part 23.____
    of a building's domestic water supply are specified by the

    A. fire department
    B. department of housing and buildings
    C. city sanitary code
    D. board of water supply

24. A housing fireman, making a preliminary inspection of a fuel oil delivery truck, discovers that the level of the oil in one compartment is far below the marker.
In this case, he SHOULD

    A. reject the shipment and order that it be returned to the terminal
    B. measure the level of the oil in the low compartment by *sticking* and report his findings to the superintendent before unloading
    C. read the liquidometer gauge before allowing the truck to be unloaded and again after it has been unloaded and record the difference in gallons to determine the amount for which payment should be made
    D. ignore the low level if it is in only one compartment

25. The *flame eye* or electronic photocell to detect a proper oil flame or flame failure is USUALLY mounted in an opening

    A. in the smoke box of the boiler
    B. in the chimney breeching in the direction of the hot gases
    C. on the front of the combustion chamber above the burner
    D. on a side wall of the furnace above the burner center line

KEY (CORRECT ANSWERS)

1.	C	11.	D
2.	B	12.	C
3.	C	13.	D
4.	D	14.	B
5.	A	15.	A
6.	C	16.	D
7.	B	17.	B
8.	B	18.	B
9.	C	19.	A
10.	B	20.	C

21. D
22. B
23. C
24. B
25. C

TEST 3

DIRECTIONS: Each question or incomplete statement is followed by several suggested answers or completions. Select the one that BEST answers the question or completes the statement. *PRINT THE LETTER OF THE CORRECT ANSWER IN THE SPACE AT THE RIGHT.*

1. The lowest visible part of the water column attached to an HRT boiler should be AT LEAST

    A. 3 inches above the top row of tubes
    B. 6 inches above the fusible plug
    C. 1 inch above the top row of tubes
    D. 1/2 inch above the fusible plug

    1.____

2. The function of a fusible plug is to

    A. melt if the water temperature is too high
    B. prevent too high a furnace temperature
    C. prevent excessive steam pressure from developing in the boiler
    D. melt when the water level drops below the level of the plug

    2.____

3. To control the temperature of water in a domestic water supply tank, the device used is USUALLY a

    A. thermostat   B. pressuretrol
    C. solenoid valve   D. aquastat

    3.____

4. A house trap is a device placed in the house drain immediately inside the foundation wall of the building.
   Its MAIN purpose is to

    A. trap sediment flowing in the house drain to the street sewer
    B. prevent sewer gases from circulating in the building plumbing system
    C. maintain air pressure balance in the vent lines of the plumbing system
    D. provide a means for cleaning the waste lines of the plumbing system

    4.____

5. In the care and operation of steam boilers, a procedure that is considered GOOD practice is to

    A. open the safety valve in the event low water is found
    B. refill the boiler with cold water when the boiler is hot
    C. remove the boiler from service immediately if the water level cannot be determined because the gauge glass is broken
    D. use hot water where possible in refilling a boiler prior to firing

    5.____

6. A sequential draft control on a rotary cup oil-fired boiler should operate to

    A. *open* the automatic damper at the end of the post-purge period
    B. *open* the automatic damper when the draft has increased during normal burner operation
    C. *close* the automatic damper just before the burner motor starts up
    D. *close* the automatic damper after the burner goes off and the burner cycle is completed

    6.____

7. The one of the following components of flue gas that indicates, when present, that more excess air is being supplied than is being used is

   A. carbon dioxide
   B. carbon monoxide
   C. nitrogen
   D. oxygen

8. An ADVANTAGE that a float-thermostatic steam trap has over a float-type steam trap of comparable rating is that a float-thermostatic trap

   A. requires less maintenance
   B. is easier to install
   C. allows non-condensable gases to escape
   D. releases the condensate at a higher temperature

9. A pump delivers 165 pounds of water per minute against a total head of 100 feet. The water horsepower of this pump is _____ HP.

   A. 1/2   B. 2   C. 5   D. 20

10. Of the following, the BEST instrument to use to measure over-the-fire draft is the

    A. Bourdon tube gauge
    B. inclined manometer
    C. mercury manometer
    D. potentiometer

11. The temperature of the water in a steam-heated domestic hot water tank is controlled by a(n)

    A. aquastat
    B. thermostatic regulating valve
    C. vacuum breaker
    D. thermostatic trap

12. If scale forms on the seat of a float-operated boiler feedwater regulator, the MOST likely result is

    A. internal corrosion of the boiler shell
    B. insufficient supply of water to the boiler
    C. flooding of the boiler
    D. shutting down of the oil burner by the low water cutout

13. The compound gauge in the oil suction line shows a high vacuum. This is USUALLY an indication of

    A. a dirty oil s.trainer
    B. low oil level in the fuel oil storage tank
    C. a leak in the fuel oil preheater
    D. an obstruction in the fuel oil preheater

14. Of the following, the information which is LEAST important on a boiler room log sheet is the

    A. stack temperature readings
    B. CO_2 readings
    C. number of boilers in operation
    D. boiler room humidity

15. Pitting and corrosion of the water side of the boiler heating surfaces is due MAINLY to the boiler water containing dissolved   15._____

    A. oxygen
    B. hydrogen
    C. soda-ash
    D. sodium sulphite

16. The combustion efficiency of a boiler can be determined with a CO_2 16._____

    A. flue gas temperature
    B. boiler room humidity
    C. outside air temperature
    D. under fire draft

17. The try-cocks of steam boilers are used to   17._____

    A. find the height of water in the boiler
    B. test steam pressure in the boiler
    C. empty the boiler of water
    D. act as safety valves

18. When a spot has burned through the fire bed, it is a GOOD plan to   18._____

    A. fill the burned out hole with green coal
    B. push burning coals to that part of the grate before spreading green coal on it
    C. fill that part of the grate with cold ashes, then place green coal on it
    D. fill the spot with excelsior and then place green coal on it

19. Thin spots or holes in a fire bed are USUALLY   19._____

    A. developed in the front part or center of the fire bed
    B. developed near the back or corners of the fire bed
    C. located where there is a smoky, dull flame
    D. the result of burning soft coal

20. With respect to the operation of univents, the custodian should   20._____

    A. close the steam valve supplying the unit radiators at the close of school every day
    B. see that the steam valve supplying the unit radiators is never closed except when repairs are required
    C. shut off the univents at the close of the day by pulling the main switch
    D. make certain that no part of the univent has water in it

21. Ventilating systems for toilets usually should be separate from the building ventilating system because   21._____

    A. it prevents toilet odors from reaching rooms
    B. toilets need a more dependable ventilating system
    C. the requirements of the two systems are different
    D. only the toilets need ventilating in summer

22. When the flues of a boiler require frequent cleaning, the PROBABLE cause is   22._____

    A. excess draft
    B. too high a rate of combustion
    C. incomplete combustion
    D. lack of clinker formation

23. Generally, the part of a school building where the HIGHEST temperature is maintained in the wintertime is the   23._____

   A. corridors
   B. toilets
   C. gymnasium
   D. regular classrooms

24. A wet return line is   24._____

   A. one containing air and water
   B. above boiler water level
   C. below boiler water level
   D. a condenser coil

25. A dry return line is   25._____

   A. one containing air *only*
   B. above boiler water level
   C. one containing air and water
   D. a line with a bleeder valve

KEY (CORRECT ANSWERS)

1.	A		11.	B
2.	D		12.	C
3.	D		13.	A
4.	B		14.	D
5.	C		15.	A
6.	D		16.	A
7.	D		17.	A
8.	C		18.	B
9.	A		19.	B
10.	B		20.	B

21. C
22. C
23. D
24. C
25. B

TEST 4

DIRECTIONS: Each question or incomplete statement is followed by several suggested answers or completions. Select the one that BEST answers the question or completes the statement. *PRINT THE LETTER OF THE CORRECT ANSWER IN THE SPACE AT THE RIGHT.*

1. The ideal flue gas temperature in a rotary cup oil-fired boiler should be equal to the steam temperature PLUS 1.____

    A. 50° F B. 125° F C. 275° F D. 550° F

2. The carbon dioxide reading in a boiler flue when the boiler is operating efficiently should be MOST NEARLY 2.____

    A. 0.5 inches of water B. 8 ounces per mol
    C. 10 psi D. 12 percent

3. The one of the following that PRIMARILY indicates a low water level in a steam boiler is the 3.____

    A. pressure gauge B. gauge glass
    C. safety valve D. hydrometer

4. The one of the following steps that should be taken FIRST if a safety valve on a coal-fired steam boiler pops off is to 4.____

    A. add water to the boiler
    B. reduce the draft
    C. tap the side of the safety valve with a mallet
    D. open the bottom blow-off valve

5. When a custodian finds that the water level of his boiler is dangerously low, he should 5.____

    A. open his drafts
    B. immediately fill boiler with cold water
    C. cover the fire with wet ashes
    D. close all air openings to the fire box

6. Which one of the following is NOT a good method in banking fires? 6.____

    A. A little ash should be left on that portion of the fire not banked.
    B. The coal should be covered with ashes to preserve the fire.
    C. The dampers should be closed except for a small opening to admit a little air.
    D. Ashes should be removed from the ashpit.

7. Radiators radiate more heat when they are painted with 7.____

    A. bronze paint B. aluminum paint
    C. regular wall paint D. shellac

8. When a boiler is laid up for the summer, one of the things NOT to do is 8.____

    A. tap brace and stary rods with a hammer to detect looserods
    B. leave water in boiler if basement is damp

C. close all hand holes and manholes to prevent dust and air from getting into the cleaned boiler
D. clean gauge glasses with muriatic acid to dissolve the accumulations of lime and other deposits

9. The safety device on a gas line is called

   A. gas cock
   B. automatic pilot
   C. solenoid valve
   D. safety shut-off valve

10. The MOST efficient boiler fuel operation is

    A. low CO_2 high CO, low stack gas temperature
    B. high CO_2 low CO, low stack gas temperature
    C. high firebox temperature, high CO_2 high stack temperature
    D. high CO_2 low CO, high stack gas temperature

11. The FIRST thing that should be checked before an oil-fired, low pressure steam boiler is started up in the morning is the

    A. boiler water level
    B. stack temperature
    C. aquastat
    D. vaporstat

12. Which of the following types of grates should be used for ease in cleaning fires when hand firing large boilers under natural draft at heavy loads with #1 buckwheat?

    A. Dumping grates
    B. Stationary grates with 3/4" air spaces
    C. Stationary grates (pinhole type)
    D. Shaking grates

13. A house pump is used to

    A. drain basements that become flooded
    B. pump sewage from the basement to the sewer
    C. pump city water to a roof storage tank
    D. circulate domestic hot water

14. The device which shuts down an automatic rotary cup oil burner when the steam pressure reaches a preset high limit is a

    A. pressure gauge
    B. pressuretrol
    C. safety valve
    D. low water cut-off

15. A pressure gauge connected to a compressed air tank USUALLY reads in

    A. pounds
    B. pounds per square inch
    C. inches of mercury
    D. feet of water

16. A badly sooted HRT boiler under coal firing will show a _____ than a clean boiler.

    A. higher CO_2 value
    B. lower CO_2 value
    C. higher stack temperature
    D. lower draft loss

17. The direct room radiator in a school with a pneumatically controlled steam treating system is cold, while the adjoining rooms are heated adequately.
    Of the following, the FIRST thing you would check in the room is the

    A. steam pipe in the room before the pneumatic steam valve
    B. thermostat
    C. pneumatic steam valve
    D. thermostatic trap

17.____

18. In the Ringelmann chart of smoke density, number 4 indicates

    A. the darkest smoke condition
    B. the lightest smoke condition
    C. smoke density of 80 percent
    D. no smoke condition

18.____

19. Of the following, the extinguishing agent that should be used on fires in flammable liquids is

    A. steam   B. water
    C. foam   D. soda and acid

19.____

20. A soda-acid fire extinguisher is recommended for use on fires consisting of

    A. wood or paper
    B. fuel oil or gasoline
    C. electrical causes or fuel oil
    D. paint or turpentine

20.____

Questions 21-23.

DIRECTIONS: Questions 21 through 23 are to be answered on the basis of the following paragraph.

A steam heating system with steam having a pressure of less than 10 pounds is called a low-pressure system. The majority of steam heating systems are of this type. The steam may be provided by low-pressure boilers installed expressly for the purpose, or it may be generated in boilers at a higher pressure and reduced in pressure before admitted to the heating mains. In other instances, it may be possible to use exhaust steam which has been made to run engines and other machines and which still contains enough heat to be utilized in the heating system. The first case represents the system of heating used in the ordinary residence or other small building; the other two represent the systems of heating employed in industrial buildings where a power plant is installed for general power purposes.

21. According to the above paragraph, whether or not a steam heating system is considered a low pressure system is determined by the pressure

    A. generated by the boiler
    B. in the heating main
    C. at the inlet side of the reducing valve
    D. of the exhaust

21.____

22. According to the above paragraph, steam used for Heating is sometimes obtained from steam   22.____

    A. generated principally to operate machinery
    B. exhausted from larger boilers
    C. generated at low pressure and brought up to high pressure before being used
    D. generated by engines other than boilers

23. As used in the above paragraph, the word *expressly* means   23.____

    A. rapidly   B. specifically
    C. usually   D. mainly

24. Of the following words, the one that is CORRECTLY spelled is   24.____

    A. suficient   B. sufficiant
    C. sufficient   D. suficiant

25. Of the following words, the one that is CORRECTLY spelled is   25.____

    A. fairly   B. fairley   C. farely   D. fairlie

KEY (CORRECT ANSWERS)

1. B		11. A
2. D		12. A
3. B		13. C
4. B		14. B
5. C		15. B
6. B		16. C
7. B		17. B
8. C		18. C
9. C		19. C
10. B		20. A

21. B
22. A
23. B
24. C
25. A

EXAMINATION SECTION
TEST 1

DIRECTIONS: Each question or incomplete statement is followed by several suggested answers or completions. Select the one that BEST answers the question or completes the statement. *PRINT THE LETTER OF THE CORRECT ANSWER IN THE SPACE AT THE RIGHT.*

1. Steam flows through pipes because of 1.____
   - A. pipe friction
   - B. superheat
   - C. pressure differences
   - D. heat circulation

2. The one of the following types of heating systems that should have an expansion tank is the _____ heating system. 2.____
   - A. one-ipe steam
   - B. hot-water
   - C. mechanical warm air
   - D. two-pipe steam

3. A Hartford Loop should be connected to a 3.____
   - A. standpipe
   - B. forced warm-air system
   - C. pipe expansion system
   - D. steam boiler

4. Whenever steam at a temperature of 230° F is to be conveyed by piping, allowances must be made for 4.____
   - A. flaring
   - B. corrosion
   - C. expansion
   - D. hardness

5. A float and thermostatic trap would MOST likely be installed in a _____ line. 5.____
   - A. fuel oil
   - B. steam heating
   - C. hot water
   - D. compressed air

6. A pipe fitting used for connecting four pipes that are at right angles to each other is called a 6.____
   - A. branch
   - B. double offset
   - C. dutchman
   - D. cross

7. An intercooler is MOST often used with a(n) 7.____
   - A. unit heater
   - B. gear type pump
   - C. oil pump
   - D. air compressor

8. A boiler bottom blow-off should be connected to the 8.____
   - A. water column
   - B. lowest water space available
   - C. superheater
   - D. steam injector

9. A boiler feedwater regulator automatically controls the 9.____
   - A. hot water temperature in the boiler
   - B. water supply to the boiler

83

C. water pressure to the boiler
D. feedwater treatment tank level

10. Steam at the temperature of evaporation is said to be

    A. saturated B. superheated
    C. dried D. exhausted

11. A unit heater supplies heat by

    A. gravity flow B. conduction
    C. forced convection D. negative pressure

12. The one of the following that is an accessory to a suspended gas unit heater is the

    A. vent B. pressure type burner
    C. drum D. fusible plug

13. A gasket material that can properly be used in oil applications is

    A. plain monel B. corrugated copper
    C. fiber D. asbestos composition

14. The one of the following that has the function of discharging the condensate from steam piping without permitting the steam to escape is a

    A. steam trap B. condenser
    C. lift valve D. poppet valve

15. The abbreviation CI stamped on the body of a valve represents a

    A. temperature limit B. seat size
    C. material designation D. service description

16. The one of the following types of valves usually used to throttle flow is the _____ valve.

    A. gate B. globe C. plug D. ball

17. The one of the following valves that should be used to maintain a constant lower pressure in a piping system delivering steam from a higher pressure source is the _____ valve.

    A. by-pass B. needle
    C. impulse D. pressure-reducing

18. A valve that will permit water to flow in one direction only is the _____ valve.

    A. blowoff B. angle C. check D. dead-end

19. The fitting that should be used to close off an opening in a pipe tee is the

    A. plug B. cowl C. eccentric D. lateral

20. Type K is a term used in connection with a

    A. lead pipe B. copper tube
    C. pipe coil D. seamless steel tank

KEY (CORRECT ANSWERS)

1. C
2. B
3. D
4. C
5. B

6. D
7. D
8. B
9. B
10. A

11. C
12. A
13. C
14. A
15. C

16. B
17. D
18. C
19. A
20. B

TEST 2

DIRECTIONS: Each question or incomplete statement is followed by several suggested answers or completions. Select the one that BEST answers the question or completes the statement. *PRINT THE LETTER OF THE CORRECT ANSWER IN THE SPACE AT THE RIGHT.*

1. In a one-pipe steam heating system, a runout to a radiator should be taken off the steam main at an angle above the horizontal of MOST NEARLY   1.____

    A. 7° B. 18° C. 30° D. 45°

2. The MINIMUM permitted size (diameter) of water column drain pipe for an industrial high pressure boiler is   2.____

    A. 3/4" B. 9/16" C. 1/2" D. 1/4"

3. The pitch of a steam main for a two-pipe high pressure system should *normally* be equal to or greater than _____ inch in ten feet.   3.____

    A. 1/4 B. 1/8 C. 1/16 D. 1/10

4. Water hammer MOST often occurs when   4.____

    A. the size of a pipe does not increase uniformly
    B. a valve is shut suddenly
    C. there is a loss of water pressure in a pipe
    D. ice forms in a pipe due to cold weather

5. One square foot of equivalent direct radiation (E.D.R.) is defined as that amount of steam-heating surface which will deliver _____ BTU per hour.   5.____

    A. 125 B. 160 C. 240 D. 295

6. When a steam radiator in a one-pipe gravity system is air bound, the cause is MOST likely to be   6.____

    A. an open steam valve   B. a defective wedge gate
    C. a defective air valve   D. insufficient steam quality

7. Of the following, the one that is MOST often the cause of *knocking* in a steam pipe is   7.____

    A. rapid expansion of the steam pipe
    B. the steam is superheated
    C. a high steam temperature
    D. reverse flow of the steam in the steam line

8. When the outside of a bare pipe is coated with moisture, the pipe is *usually* carrying   8.____

    A. hot water   B. steam
    C. cold water   D. hot gas

9. *Pipe schedule number 80* refers to a pipe that is classified as   9.____

    A. double extra strong   B. type M
    C. extra strong   D. standard

10. The one of the following that is *generally* used to anchor a pipe support bracket to a concrete wall is the

    A. shackle
    B. blivet
    C. expansion shield
    D. mullion

11. A recess in the wall of a building, for the purpose of holding pipes which go from floor to floor, is called a

    A. closet B. bidet C. chase D. cowl

12. The one of the following that can be used as an escutcheon is the

    A. flange B. union C. cap D. leader

13. The one of the following types of valves that should be used when very accurate throttling is required is the _____ valve.

    A. relief B. poppet C. lift D. needle

14. The letters O. S. and Y. are abbreviations for

    A. outside size wye
    B. operating shock service
    C. outside screw and yoke
    D. operating steam yoke

15. The symbols *150 SP* on a valve represent the valve's

    A. air capacity
    B. rating
    C. water capacity
    D. maintenance

16. The one of the following devices that is sensitive to changes in air temperature in a room is the

    A. rheostat
    B. thermostat
    C. damperstat
    D. aquastat

17. The *nominal* size of a 3-inch pipe refers to the pipe's

    A. inside diameter
    B. wall thickness
    C. weight per foot
    D. root diameter

18. Brass is basically made of copper and

    A. tungsten B. antimony C. lead D. zinc

19. A metal formed by the combination of two or more metals is known as an

    A. anneal B. extrusion C. element D. alloy

20. The MAIN element in a ferrous metal is

    A. iron B. cadmium C. copper D. bismuth

KEY (CORRECT ANSWERS)

1.	D	11.	C
2.	A	12.	A
3.	A	13.	D
4.	B	14.	C
5.	C	15.	B
6.	C	16.	B
7.	A	17.	A
8.	C	18.	D
9.	C	19.	D
10.	C	20.	A

READING COMPREHENSION
UNDERSTANDING AND INTERPRETING WRITTEN MATERIAL
EXAMINATION SECTION
TEST 1

DIRECTIONS: Each question or incomplete statement is followed by several suggested answers or completions. Select the one that BEST answers the question or completes the statement. *PRINT THE LETTER OF THE CORRECT ANSWER IN THE SPACE AT THE RIGHT.*

Questions 1-2.

DIRECTIONS: Questions 1 and 2 are to be answered SOLELY on the basis of the following paragraph.

When fixing an upper sash cord, you must also remove the lower sash. To do this, the parting strip between the sash must be removed. Now remove the cover from the weight box channel, cut off the cord as before, and pull it over the pulleys. Pull your new cord over the pulleys and down into the channel where it may be fastened to the weight. The cord for an upper sash is cut off 1" or 2" below the pulley with the weight resting on the floor of the pocket and the cord held taut. These measurements allow for slight stretching of the cord. When the cord is cut to length, it can be pulled up over the pulley and tied with a single common knot in the end to fit into the socket in the sash groove. If the knot protrudes beyond the face of the sash, tap it gently to flatten. In this way, it will not become frayed from constant rubbing against the groove.

1. When repairing the upper sash cord, the FIRST thing to do is to
   A. remove the lower sash
   B. cut the existing sash cord
   C. remove the parting strip
   D. measure the length of new cord necessary

1._____

2. According to the above paragraph, the rope may become frayed if the
   A. pulley is too small   B. knot sticks out
   C. cord is too long   D. weight is too heavy

2._____

Questions 3-4.

DIRECTIONS: Questions 3 and 4 are to be answered SOLELY on the basis of the following paragraph.

Repeated burning of the same area should be avoided. Burning should not be done on impervious, shallow, unstable, or highly erodible soils, or on steep slopes—especially in areas subject to heavy rains or rapid snowmelt. When existing vegetation is likely to be killed or seriously weakened by the fire, measures should be taken to assure prompt revegetation of the burned area. Burns should be limited to relatively small proportions of a watershed unit so that the stream channels will be able to carry any increased flows with a minimum of damage.

3. According to the above paragraph, planned burning should be limited to small areas of the watershed because
    A. the fire can be better controlled
    B. existing vegetation will be less likely to be killed
    C. plants will grow quicker in small areas
    D. there will be less likelihood of damaging floods

3._____

4. According to the above paragraph, burning USUALLY should be done on soils that
    A. readily absorb moisture
    B. have been burnt before
    C. exist as a thin layer over rock
    D. can be flooded by nearby streams

4._____

Questions 5-11.

DIRECTIONS: Questions 5 through 11 are to be answered SOLELY on the basis of the following paragraph.

FUSE INFORMATION

Badly bent or distorted fuse clips cannot be permitted. Sometimes, the distortion or bending is so slight that it escapes notice, yet it may be the cause for fuse failures through the heat that is developed by the poor contact. Occasionally, the proper spring tension of the fuse clips has been destroyed by overheating from loose wire connections to the clips. Proper contact surfaces must be maintained to avoid faulty operation of the fuse. Maintenance men should remove oxides that form on the copper and brass contacts, check the clip pressure, and make sure that contact surfaces are not deformed or bent in any way. When removing oxides, use a well-worn file and remove only the oxide film. Do not use sandpaper or emery cloth as hard particles may come off and become embedded in the contact surfaces. All wire connections to the fuse holders should be carefully inspected to see that they are tight.

5. Fuse failure because of poor clip contact or loose connections is due to the resulting
    A. excessive voltage   B. increased current
    C. lowered resistance   D. heating effect

5._____

6. Oxides should be removed from fuse contacts by using
    A. a dull file   B. emery cloth
    C. fine sandpaper   D. a sharp file

6._____

7. One result of loose wire connections at the terminal of a fuse clip is stated in the above paragraph to be
    A. loss of tension in the wire
    B. welding of the fuse to the clip
    C. distortion of the clip
    D. loss of tension of the clip

7._____

8. Simple reasoning will show that the oxide film referred to is undesirable CHIEFLY because it	8._____
   A. looks dull
   B. makes removal of the fuse difficult
   C. weakens the clips
   D. introduces undesirable resistance

9. Fuse clips that are bent very slightly	9._____
   A. should be replaced with new clips
   B. should be carefully filed
   C. may result in blowing of the fuse
   D. may prevent the fuse from blowing

10. From the fuse information paragraph, it would be reasonable to conclude that fuse clips	10._____
    A. are difficult to maintain
    B. must be given proper maintenance
    C. require more attention than other electrical equipment
    D. are unreliable

11. A safe practical way of checking the tightness of the wire connection to the fuse clips of a live 120-volt lighting circuit is to	11._____
    A. feel the connection with your hand to see if it is warm
    B. try tightening with an insulated screwdriver or socket wrench
    C. see if the circuit works
    D. measure the resistance with an ohmmeter

Questions 12-13.

DIRECTIONS: Questions 12 through 13 are to be answered SOLELY on the basis of the following paragraph.

For cast iron pipe lines, the middle ring or sleeve shall have *beveled* ends and shall be high quality cast iron. The middle ring shall have a minimum wall thickness of 3/8" for pipe up to 8", 7/16" for pipe 10" to 30", and 1/2" for pipe over 30", nominal diameter. Minimum length of middle ring shall be 5" for pipe up to 10", 6" for pipe 10" to 30", and 10" for pipe 30" nominal diameter and larger. The middle ring shall not have a center pipe stop, unless otherwise specified.

12. As used in the above paragraph, the word *beveled* means MOST NEARLY	12._____
    A. straight   B. slanted   C. curved   D. rounded

13. In accordance with the above paragraph, the middle ring of a 24" nominal diameter pipe would have a minimum wall thickness and length of _____ thick and _____ long.	13._____
    A. 3/8"; 5:   B. 3/8"; 6"
    C. 7/16"; 6"   D. 1/2"; 6"

Questions 14-17.

DIRECTIONS: Questions 14 through 17 are to be answered SOLELY on the basis of the following paragraph.

Operators spotting loads with long booms and working around men need the smooth, easy operation and positive control of uniform pressure swing clutches. There are no jerks or grabs with these large disc-type clutches because there is always even pressure over the entire clutch lining surface. In the conventional band-type swing clutch, the pressure varies between dead and live ends of the band. The uniform pressure swing clutch has excellent provision for heat dissipation. The driving elements, which are always rotating, have a great number of fins cast in them. This gives them an impeller or blower action for cooling, resulting in longer life and freedom from frequent adjustment.

14. According to the above paragraph, it may be said that conventional band-type swing clutches have
    A. even pressure on the clutch lining
    B. larger contact area
    C. smaller contact area
    D. uneven pressure on the clutch lining

15. According to the above paragraph, machines equipped with uniform pressure swing clutches will
    A. give better service under all conditions
    B. require no clutch adjustment
    C. give positive control of hoist
    D. provide better control of swing

16. According to the above paragraph, it may be said that the rotation of the driving elements of the uniform pressure swing clutch is ALWAYS
    A. continuous
    B. constant
    C. varying
    D. uncertain

17. According to the above paragraph, freedom from frequent adjustment is due to the
    A. operator's smooth, easy operation
    B. positive control of the clutch
    C. cooling effect of the rotating fins
    D. larger contact area of the bigger clutch

Questions 18-22.

DIRECTIONS: Questions 18 through 22 are to be answered SOLELY on the basis of the following paragraphs.

Exhaust valve clearance adjustment on diesel engines is very important for proper operation of the engine. Insufficient clearance between the exhaust valve stem and the rocker arm causes a loss of compression and, after a while, burning of the valves and valve seat inserts. On the other hand, too much valve clearance will result in noisy operation of the engine.

Exhaust valves that are maintained in good operating condition will result in efficient combustion in the engine. Valve seats must be true and unpitted, and valve stems must work smoothly within the valve guides. Long valve life will result from proper maintenance and operation of the engine.

Engine operating temperatures should be maintained between 160°F and 185°F. Low operating temperatures result in incomplete combustion and the deposit of fuel lacquers on valves.

18. According to the above paragraphs, too much valve clearance will cause the engine to operate 18._____
    A. slowly   B. noisily   C. smoothly   D. cold

19. On the basis of the information given in the above paragraphs, operating temperatures of a diesel engine should be between 19._____
    A. 125°F and 130°F   B. 140°F and 150°F
    C. 160°F and 185°F   D. 190°F and 205°F

20. According to the above paragraphs, the deposit of fuel lacquers on valves is caused by 20._____
    A. high operating temperatures
    B. insufficient valve clearance
    C. low operating temperatures
    D. efficient combustion

21. According to the above paragraphs, for efficient operation of the engine, valve seats must 21._____
    A. have sufficient clearance
    B. be true and unpitted
    C. operate at low temperatures
    D. be adjusted regularly

22. According to the above paragraphs, a loss of compression is due to insufficient clearance between the exhaust valve stem and the 22._____
    A. rocker arm   B. valve seat
    C. valve seat inserts D. valve guides

Questions 23-25.

DIRECTIONS: Questions 23 through 25 are to be answered SOLELY on the basis of the following excerpt:

A SPECIFICATION FOR ELECTRIC WORK FOR THE CITY

Breakers shall be equipped with magnetic blowout coils...Handles of breakers shall be trip-free...Breakers shall be designed to carry 100% of trip rating continuously; to have inverse time delay tripping above 100% of trip rating...

23. According to the above paragraph, the breaker shall have provision for 23._____
    A. resetting   B. arc quenching
    C. adjusting trip time D. adjusting trip rating

24. According to the above paragraph, the breaker 24._____
    A. shall trip easily at exactly 100% of trip rating
    B. shall trip instantly at a little more than 100% of trip rating
    C. should be constructed so that it shall not be possible to prevent it from opening on overload or short circuit by holding the handle in the ON position
    D. shall not trip prematurely at 100% of trip rating

25. According to the above paragraph, the breaker shall trip
    A. instantaneously as soon as 100% of trip rating is reached
    B. instantaneously as soon as 100% of trip rating is exceeded
    C. more quickly the greater the current, once 100% of trip rating is exceeded
    D. after a predetermined fixed time lapse, once 100% of trip rating is reached

25.____

KEY (CORRECT ANSWERS)

1.	C		11.	B
2.	B		12.	B
3.	D		13.	C
4.	A		14.	D
5.	D		15.	D
6.	A		16.	A
7.	D		17.	C
8.	D		18.	B
9.	C		19.	C
10.	B		20.	C

21.	B
22.	A
23.	B
24.	C
25.	C

TEST 2

DIRECTIONS: Each question or incomplete statement is followed by several suggested answers or completions. Select the one that BEST answers the question or completes the statement. *PRINT THE LETTER OF THE CORRECT ANSWER IN THE SPACE AT THE RIGHT.*

Questions 1-4.

DIRECTIONS: Questions 1 through 4 are to be answered SOLELY on the basis of the following paragraph.

A low pressure hot water boiler shall include a relief valve or valves of a capacity such that with the heat generating equipment operating at maximum, the pressure cannot rise more than 20 percent above the maximum allowable working pressure (set pressure) if that is 30 p.s.i. gage or less, nor more than 10 percent if it is more than 30 p.s.i. gage. The difference between the set pressure and the pressure at which the valve is relieving is known as *over-pressure or accumulation.* If the steam relieving capacity in pounds per hour is calculated, it shall be determined by dividing by 1,000 the maximum BTU output at the boiler nozzle obtainable from the heat generating equipment, or by multiplying the square feet of heating surface by five.

1. In accordance with the above paragraph, the capacity of a relief valve should be computed on the basis of
    A. size of boiler
    B. maximum rated capacity of generating equipment
    C. average output of the generating equipment
    D. minimum capacity of generating equipment

1._____

2. In accordance with the above paragraph, with a set pressure of 30 p.s.i. gage, the overpressure should not be more than _____ p.s.i.
    A. 3   B. 6   C. 33   D. 36

2._____

3. In accordance with the above paragraph, a relief valve should start relieving at a pressure equal to the
    A. set pressure
    B. over pressure
    C. over pressure minus set pressure
    D. set pressure plus over pressure

3._____

4. In accordance with the above paragraph, the steam relieving capacity can be computed by
    A. *multiplying* the maximum BTU output by 5
    B. *dividing* the pounds of steam per hour by 1,000
    C. *dividing* the maximum BTU output by the square feet of heating surface
    D. *dividing* the maximum BTU output by 1,000

4._____

Questions 5-8.

DIRECTIONS: Questions 5 through 8 are to be answered SOLELY on the basis of the following paragraph.

Air conditioning units requiring a minimum rate of flow of water in excess of one-half (1/2) gallon per minute shall be metered. Air conditioning equipment with a refrigeration unit which has a definite rate of capacity in tons or fractions thereof, the charge will be at the rate of $30 per annum per ton capacity from the date installed to the date when the supply is metered. Such units, when equipped with an approved water-conserving device, shall be charged at the rate of $4.50 per annum per ton capacity from the date installed to the date when the supply is metered.

5. A man who was in the market for air conditioning equipment was considering three different units. Unit 1 required a flow of 28 gallons of water per hour; Unit 2 required 30 gallons of water per hour; Unit 3 required 32 gallons of water per hour. The man asked the salesman which units would require the installation of a water meter. According to the above passage, the salesman SHOULD answer:
   A. All three units require meters
   B. Units 2 and 3 require meters
   C. Unit 3 only requires a meter
   D. None of the units require a meter

5._____

6. Suppose that air conditioning equipment with a refrigeration unit of 10 tons was put in operation on October 1; and in the following year on July 1, a meter was installed. According to the above passage, the charge for this period would be _____ the annual rate.
   A. twice   B. equal to
   C. three-fourths   D. one-fourth

6._____

7. The charge for air conditioning equipment which has no refrigeration unit
   A. is $30 per year
   B. is $25.50 per year
   C. is $4.50 per year
   D. cannot be determined from the above passage

7._____

8. The charge for air conditioning equipment with a seven-ton refrigeration unit equipped with an approved water-conserving device
   A. is $4.50 per year
   B. is $25.50 per year
   C. is $31.50 per year
   D. cannot be determined from the above passage

8._____

Questions 9-14.

DIRECTIONS: Questions 9 through 14 are to be answered SOLELY on the basis of the following paragraph.

The city makes unremitting efforts to keep the water free from pollution. An inspectional force under a sanitary expert is engaged in patrolling the watersheds to see that the department's sanitary regulations are observed. Samples taken daily from various points in the water supply system are examined and analyzed at the three laboratories maintained by the department. All water before delivery to the distribution mains is treated with chlorine to destroy bacteria. In addition, some water is aerated to free it from gases and, in some cases, from microscopic organisms. Generally, microscopic organisms which develop in the reservoirs and at times impart an unpleasant taste and odor to the water, though in no sense harmful to health, are destroyed by treatment with copper sulfate and by chlorine dosage. None of the supplies is filtered, but the quality of the water supplied by the city is excellent for all purposes, and it is clear and wholesome.

9. According to the above paragraph, microscopic organisms are removed from the water supplied to the city by means of   9._____
   A. chlorine alone
   B. chlorine, aeration, and filtration
   C. chlorine, aeration, filtration, and sampling
   D. copper sulfate, chlorine, and aeration

10. Microscopic organisms in the water supply GENERALLY are   10._____
    A. a health menace   B. impossible to detect
    C. not harmful to health D. not destroyed in the water

11. The MAIN function of the inspectional force, as described in the above paragraph, is to   11._____
    A. take samples of water for analysis
    B. enforce sanitary regulations
    C. add chlorine to the water supply
    D. inspect water-use meters

12. According to the above paragraph, chlorine is added to water before entering the   12._____
    A. watersheds   B. reservoirs
    C. distribution mains D. run-off areas

13. Of the following suggested headings or titles for the above paragraph, the one that BEST tells what the paragraph is about is   13._____
    A. QUALITY OF WATER   B. CHLORINATION OF WATER
    C. TESTING OF WATER   D. BACTERIA IN WATER

14. The MOST likely reason for taking samples of water for examination and analysis from various points in the water supply system is: 14._____
    A. The testing points are convenient to the department's laboratories
    B. Water from one part of the system may be made undrinkable by a local condition
    C. The samples can be distributed equally among the three laboratories
    D. The hardness or softness of water varies from place to place

Questions 15-17.

DIRECTIONS: Questions 15 through 17 are to be answered SOLELY on the basis of the following paragraph.

A building measuring 200' x 100' at the street is set back 20' on all sides at the 15th floor, and an additional 10' on all sides at the 30th floor. The building is 35 stories high.

15. The floor area of the 16th floor is MOST NEARLY _____ sq. ft. 15._____
    A. 20,000   B. 14,400   C. 9,600   D. 7,500

16. The floor area of the 35th floor is MOST NEARLY _____ sq. ft. 16._____
    A. 20,000   B. 13,900   C. 7,500   D. 5,600

17. The floor area of the 16th floor, compared to the floor area of the 2nd floor, is MOST NEARLY _____ as much. 17._____
    A. three-fourths (3/4)   B. two-thirds (2/3)
    C. one-half (1/2)   D. four-tenths (4/10)

Question 18.

DIRECTIONS: Question 18 is to be answered SOLELY on the basis of the following paragraph.

Experience has shown that, in general, a result of the installation of meters on services not previously metered is to reduce the amount of water consumed, but is not necessarily to reduce the peak load on plumbing systems. The permissible head loss through meters at their rated maximum flow is 20 p.s.i. The installation of a meter may therefore appreciably lower the pressures available in fixtures on a plumbing system.

18. According to the above paragraph, a water meter may 18._____
    A. limit the flow in the plumbing system of 20 p.s.i.
    B. reduce the peak load on the plumbing system
    C. increase the overall amount of water consumed
    D. reduce the pressure in the plumbing system

Question 19.

DIRECTIONS: Question 19 is to be answered SOLELY on the basis of the following paragraph.

Spring comes without trumpets to a city. The asphalt is a wilderness that does not quicken overnight; winds blow gritty with cinders instead of merry with the smells of earth and fertilizer. Women wear their gardens on their hats. But spring is a season in the city, and it has its own harbingers, constant as daffodils. Shop windows change their colors, people walk more slowly on the streets, what one can see of the sky has a bluer tone. Pulitzer prizes awake and sing and matinee tickets go-a-begging. But gayer than any of these are the carousels, which are already in sheltered places, beginning to turn with the sound of springtime itself. They are the earliest and the truest and the oldest of all the urban signs.

19. In the passage above, the word *harbingers* means 19._____
    A. storms   B. truths   C. virtues   D. forerunners

Questions 20-22.

DIRECTIONS: Questions 20 through 22 are to be answered SOLELY on the basis of the following paragraph.

Gas heaters include manually operated, automatic, and instantaneous heaters. Some heaters are equipped with a thermostat which controls the fuel supply so that when the water falls below a predetermined temperature, the fuel is automatically turned on. In some types, the hot-water storage tank is well-insulated to economize the use of fuel. Instantaneous heaters are arranged so that the opening of a faucet on the hot-water pipe will increase the flow of fuel, which is ignited by a continuously burning pilot light to heat the water to from 120° to 130°F. The possibility that the pilot light will die out offers a source of danger in the use of automatic appliances which depend on a pilot light. Gas and oil heaters are dangerous, and they should be designed to prevent the accumulation, in a confined space within the heater, of a large volume of an explosive mixture.

20. According to the above passage, the opening of a hot-water faucet on a hot-water pipe connected to an instantaneous hot-water heater will the pilot light.
    A. *increase* the temperature of
    B. *increase* the flow of fuel to
    C. *decrease* the flow of fuel to
    D. *have a marked effect* on

21. According to the above passage, the fuel is automatically turned on in a heater equipped with a thermostat whenever
    A. the water temperature drops below 120°F
    B. the pilot light is lit
    C. the water temperature drops below some predetermined temperature
    D. a hot water supply is opened

22. According to the above passage, some hot-water storage tanks are well-insulated to
    A. accelerate the burning of the fuel
    B. maintain the water temperature between 120° and 130°F
    C. prevent the pilot light from being extinguished
    D. minimize the expenditure of fuel

Question 23.

DIRECTIONS: Question 23 is to be answered SOLELY on the basis of the following paragraph.

Breakage of the piston under high-speed operation has been the commonest fault of disc piston meters. Various techniques are adopted to prevent this, such as *throttling* the meter, cutting away the edge of the piston, or reinforcing it, but these are simply makeshifts.

23. As used in the above paragraph, the word *throttling* means MOST NEARLY
    A. enlarging   B. choking
    C. harnessing   D. dismantling

Questions 24-25.

DIRECTIONS: Questions 24 and 25 are to be answered SOLELY on the basis of the following paragraph.

One of the most common and objectionable difficulties occurring in a drainage system is trap seal loss. This failure can be attributed directly to inadequate ventilation of the trap and the subsequent negative and positive pressures which occur. A trap seal may be lost either by siphonage and/or back pressure. Loss of the trap seal by siphonage is the result of a negative pressure in the drainage system. The seal content of the trap is forced by siphonage into the waste piping of the drainage system through exertion of atmospheric pressure on the fixture side of the trap seal.

24. According to the above paragraph, a positive pressure is a direct result of
    A. siphonage
    B. unbalanced trap seal
    C. poor ventilation
    D. atmospheric pressure

25. According to the above paragraph, the water in the trap is forced into the drain pipe by
    A. atmospheric pressure
    B. back pressure
    C. negative pressure
    D. back pressure on fixture side of seal

KEY (CORRECT ANSWERS)

1. B
2. B
3. D
4. D
5. C

6. C
7. D
8. C
9. D
10. C

11. B
12. C
13. A
14. B
15. C

16. D
17. C
18. D
19. B
20. B

21. C
22. D
23. B
24. C
25. A

ARITHMETICAL REASONING
EXAMINATION SECTION
TEST 1

DIRECTIONS: Each question or incomplete statement is followed by several suggested answers or completions. Select the one that BEST answers the question or completes the statement. *PRINT THE LETTER OF THE CORRECT ANSWER IN THE SPACE AT THE RIGHT.*

1.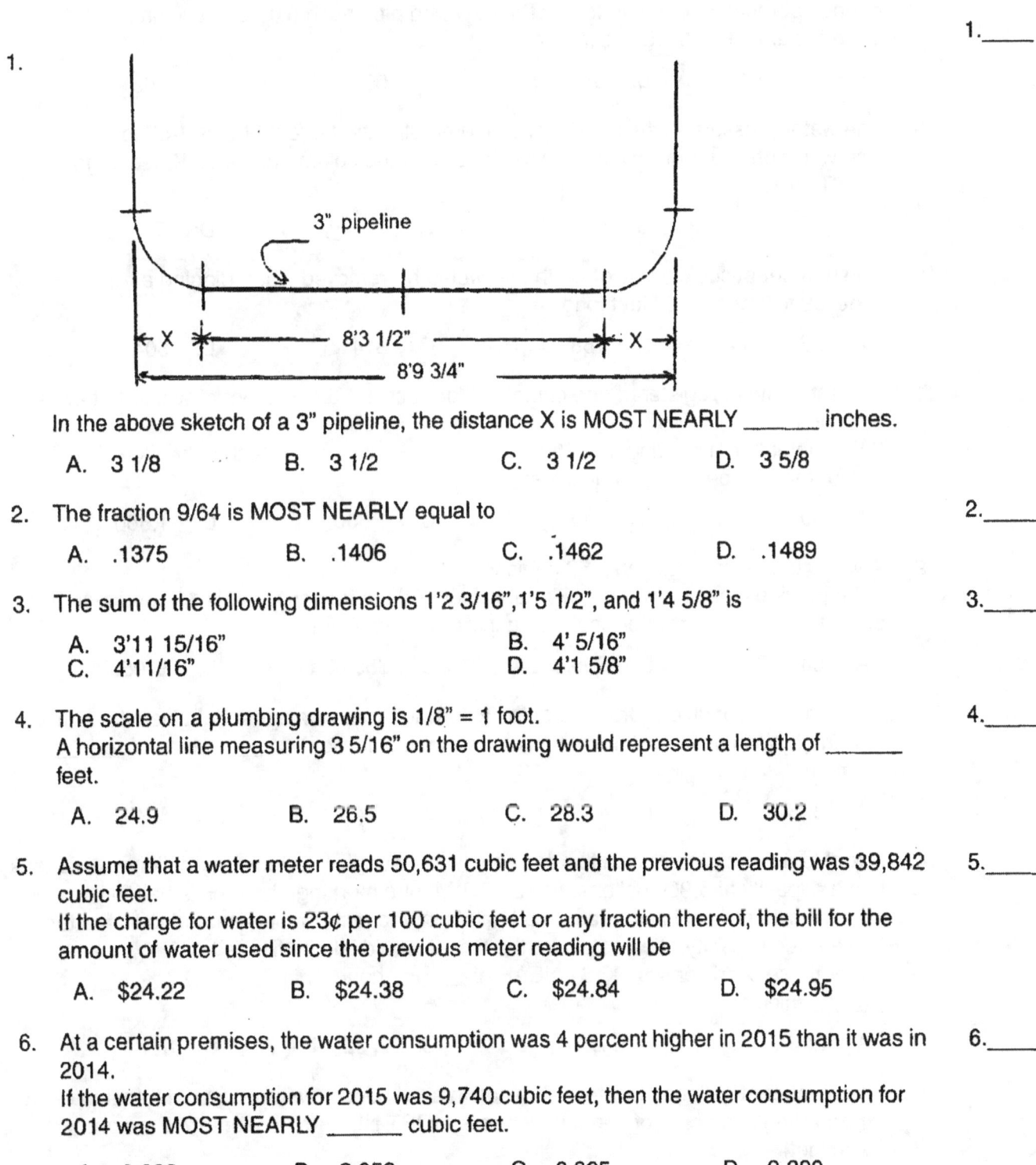

   In the above sketch of a 3" pipeline, the distance X is MOST NEARLY _____ inches.

   A. 3 1/8   B. 3 1/2   C. 3 1/2   D. 3 5/8

2. The fraction 9/64 is MOST NEARLY equal to

   A. .1375   B. .1406   C. .1462   D. .1489

3. The sum of the following dimensions 1'2 3/16", 1'5 1/2", and 1'4 5/8" is

   A. 3'11 15/16"   B. 4' 5/16"
   C. 4'11/16"   D. 4'1 5/8"

4. The scale on a plumbing drawing is 1/8" = 1 foot.
   A horizontal line measuring 3 5/16" on the drawing would represent a length of _____ feet.

   A. 24.9   B. 26.5   C. 28.3   D. 30.2

5. Assume that a water meter reads 50,631 cubic feet and the previous reading was 39,842 cubic feet.
   If the charge for water is 23¢ per 100 cubic feet or any fraction thereof, the bill for the amount of water used since the previous meter reading will be

   A. $24.22   B. $24.38   C. $24.84   D. $24.95

6. At a certain premises, the water consumption was 4 percent higher in 2015 than it was in 2014.
   If the water consumption for 2015 was 9,740 cubic feet, then the water consumption for 2014 was MOST NEARLY _____ cubic feet.

   A. 9,320   B. 9,350   C. 9,365   D. 9,390

7. A pump delivers water at a constant rate of 40 gallons per minute.
If there are 7.5 gallons to a cubic foot of water, the time it will take to fill a tank 6 feet x 5 feet x 4 feet is MOST NEARLY _____ minutes.

   A. 15　　B. 22.5　　C. 28.5　　D. 30

8. The total weight, in pounds, of three lengths of 3" cast-iron pipe 7'6" long, weighing 14.5 pounds per foot, and four lengths of 4" cast-iron pipe each 5'0" long, weighing 13.0 pounds per foot, is MOST NEARLY

   A. 540　　B. 585　　C. 600　　D. 665

9. The water pressure at the bottom of a column of water 34 feet high is 14.7 lbs./sq.in. The water pressure in lbs./sq.in. at the bottom of the column of water 12 feet high is MOST NEARLY

   A. 3　　B. 5　　C. 7　　D. 9

10. The number of cubic yards of earth that would be removed when digging a trench 8 feet wide x 9 feet deep x 63 feet long is

    A. 56　　B. 168　　C. 314　　D. 504

11. On test, a meter registered one cubic foot for each 1 1/3 cubic feet of water that passed through it.
If the meter had a reading of 1,200 cubic feet, we may conclude that the CORRECT amount should be _____ cubic feet.

    A. 800　　B. 900　　C. 1,500　　D. 1,600

12. A water use meter reads 87,463 cubic feet.
If the previous reading was 17,377 cubic feet and the rate charged is 15 cents per 100 cubic feet, the bill for water use during this period is about

    A. $45.00　　B. $65.00　　C. $85.00　　D. $105.00

13. Under proper conditions, the one of the following groups of pipes that gives the same flow in gals/min as one 6" diameter pipe is (neglect friction) _____ pipes of _____ diameter each.

    A. 3; 3"　　B. 4; 3"　　C. 2; 4"　　D. 3; 4"

14. A roof tank is used to furnish the domestic water supply to a ten story building. This tank has a capacity of 5,900 gallons. At 10:00 A.M. one morning, the tank is half full.
If water is being used at the rate of 50 gals/min, the pump which is used to fill the tank has a rated capacity of 90 gals/min, the time it would take to fill the tank under these conditions is MOST NEARLY _____ hour(s), _____ minutes.

    A. 2; 8　　B. 1; 14　　C. 2; 32　　D. 1; 2

15. The number of gallons of water contained in a cylindrical swimming pool 8 feet in diameter and filled to a depth of 3 feet 6 inches is MOST NEARLY (assume 7.5 gallons = 1 cubic foot)

    A. 30　　B. 225　　C. 1,320　　D. 3,000

16. The charge for metered water is 52 1/2 cents per hundred cubic feet, with a minimum charge of $21 per annum. Of the following, the SMALLEST water usage in hundred cubic feet that would result in a charge GREATER than the minimum is

    A. 39   B. 40   C. 41   D. 42

17. The annual frontage rent on a one-story building 40 ft. in length is $735.00. For each additional story, $52.50 per annum is added to the frontage rent. For demolition, the charge for wetting down is 3/8 of the annual frontage charge.
    The charge for wetting down a building six stories in height, with a 40 ft. frontage, is MOST NEARLY

    A. $369   B. $371   C. $372   D. $374

18. If the drawing of a piping layout is made to a scale of 1/4" equals one foot, then a 7'9" length of piping would be represented by a scaled length on the drawing of APPROXIMATELY _____ inches.

    A. 2   B. 7 3/4   C. 23 1/4   D. 31

19. A plumbing sketch is drawn to a scale of eighth-size. A line measuring 3" on the sketch would be equivalent to _____ feet.

    A. 2   B. 6   C. 12   D. 24

20. If 500 feet of pipe weighs 800 lbs., the number of pounds that 120 feet will weigh is MOST NEARLY

    A. 190   B. 210   C. 230   D. 240

21. If a trench is excavated 3'0" wide by 5'6" deep and 50 feet long, the total number of cubic yards of earth removed is MOST NEARLY

    A. 30   B. 90   C. 150   D. 825

22. Assume that a plumber earns $86,500 per year.
    If eighteen percent of his pay is deducted for taxes and social security, his net weekly pay will be APPROXIMATELY

    A. $1,326   B. $1,365   C. $1,436   D. $1,457.50

23. Assume that a plumbing installation is made up of the following fixtures and groups of fixtures: 12 bathroom groups each containing one W.C., one lavatory, and one bathtub with shower; 12 bathroom groups each containing one W.C., one lavatory, one bathtub, and one shower stall; 24 combination kitchen fixtures; 4 floor drains; 6 slop sinks without flushing rim; and 2 shower stalls (or shower bath).
    The total number of fixtures for the above plumbing installation is MOST NEARLY

    A. 60   B. 95   C. 120   D. 210

24. A triangular opening in a wall forms a 30-60 degree right triangle.
    If the longest side measures 12'0", then the shortest side will measure

    A. 3'0"   B. 4'0"   C. 6'0"   D. 8'0"

25. You are directed to cut 4 pieces of pipe, one each of the following length: 2'6 1/4", 3'9 3/8", 4'7 5/8", and 5'8 7/8".
    The total length of these 4 pieces is

    A. 15'7 1/4"   B. 15'9 3/8"   C. 16'5 7/8"   D. 16'8 1/8"

25._____

KEY (CORRECT ANSWERS)

1. A	11. D
2. B	12. D
3. B	13. B
4. B	14. B
5. C	15. C
6. C	16. C
7. B	17. D
8. B	18. A
9. B	19. A
10. B	20. A

21. A
22. B
23. C
24. C
25. D

SOLUTIONS TO PROBLEMS

1. 8'3 1/2" + x + x = 8'9 3/4" Then, 2x = 6 1/4", so x = 3 1/8"

2. 9/64 = .140625 = .1406

3. 1'2 3/16" + 1'5 1/2" +1'4 5/8" = 3'11 21/16" = 4'5/16"

4. 3 5/16" ÷ 1/8" =53/16 x 8/1 = 26.5. Then, (26.5)(1 ft.) = 26.5 feet

5. 50,631 - 39,842 = 10,789; 10,789 ÷ 100 = 107.89
   Since the cost is .23 per 100 cubic feet or any fraction thereof, the cost will be
   (.23)(107) + .23 = $24.84

6. 9740 ÷ 1.04 = 9365 cu.ft.

7. 40 ÷ 7.5 = 5 1/3 cu.ft. of water per minute. The volume = (6)(5)(4) = 120 cu.ft. Thus, the number of minutes needed to fill the tank is 120 ÷ 5 1/3 = 22.5

8. 3" pipe: 3 x 7'6" = 22 1/2' x 14.5 lbs. = 326.25
   4" pipe: 4 x 5' = 20' x 13 lbs. = 260
   326.25 + 260 = 586.25 (most nearly 585)

9. Let x = pressure. Then, 34/12 = 14.7/x. So, 34x = 176.4
   Solving, x ≈ 5 lbs./sq.in.

10. (8)(9)(63) = 4536 cu.ft. Since 1 cu.yd. = 27 cu.ft., 4536 cu.ft. is equivalent to 168 cu.yds.

11. Let x = correct amount. Then, $\frac{1}{1200} = \frac{1\frac{1}{3}}{x}$. Solving, x = 1600

12. 87,463 - 17,377 = 70,086; and 70,086 ÷ 100 = 700.86 ≈ 700 Then, (700)(.15) = $105.00

13. Cross-sectional area of a 6" diameter pipe = (π)(3")^2 = 9π sq. in. Note that the combined cross-sectional areas of four 3" diameter pipes = (4)(π)(1.5")^2 = 9π sq. in.

14. 90 - 50 = 40 gals/min. Then, 2950 ÷ 40 = 73.75 min. ≈ 1 hr. 14 min.

15. Volume = (π)(4)^2(3 1/2) = 56π cu.ft. Then, (56π)(7.5) = 1320 gals.

16. For 4100 cu.ft., the charge of (.525)(41) = $21,525 > $21

17. Rent = $73,500 + (5)($52.50) = $997,50. For demolition, the charge = (3/8)($997.50)
    $374

18. (1/4")(7.75) = 2"

19. (3")(8) = 24" = 2 ft.

20. Let x = weight. Then, 500/800 = 120/x . Solving, x = 192 190 lbs.

21. (3')(5 1/2')(50') = 825 cu.ft. Then, 825 ÷ 27 ≈ 30 cu.yds.

22. Net pay = (.82)($86,500) = $70,930/yr. Weekly pay = $70,930 ÷ 52 ≈ $1365

23. (12x3) + (12x4) +24+4+6+2= 120

24. The shortest side = (1/2)(hypotenuse) = (1/2)(12') = 6'

25. 2'6 1/4" + 3'9 3/8" + 4'7 5/8" + 5'8 7/8 " = 14'30 17/8" = 16'8 1/8"

TEST 2

DIRECTIONS: Each question or incomplete statement is followed by several suggested answers or completions. Select the one that BEST answers the question or completes the statement. *PRINT THE LETTER OF THE CORRECT ANSWER IN THE SPACE AT THE RIGHT.*

1. The sum of the following pipe lengths, 15 5/8", 8 3/4", 30 5/16" and 20 1/2", is   1.____

   A. 77 1/8"   B. 76 3/16"   C. 75 3/16"   D. 74 5/16"

2. If the outside diameter of a pipe is 6 inches and the wall thickness is 1/2 inch, the inside area of this pipe, in square inches, is MOST NEARLY   2.____

   A. 15.7   B. 17.3   C. 19.6   D. 23.8

3. Three lengths of pipe 1'10", 3'2 1/2", and 5'7 1/2", respectively, are to be cut from a pipe 14'0" long.   3.____
   Allowing 1/8" for each pipe cut, the length of pipe remaining is

   A. 3'1 1/8"   B. 3'2 1/2"   C. 3'3 1/4"   D. 3'3 5/8"

4. According to the building code, the MAXIMUM permitted surface temperature of combustible construction materials located near heating equipment is 76.5°C. (°F=(°Cx9/5)+32) Maximum temperature Fahrenheit is MOST NEARLY   4.____

   A. 170° F   B. 195° F   C. 210° F   D. 220° F

5. A pump discharges 7.5 gals/minutes.   5.____
   In 2.5 hours the pump will discharge _____ gallons.

   A. 1125   B. 1875   C. 1950   D. 2200

6. A pipe with an outside diameter of 4" has a circumference of MOST NEARLY _____ inches.   6.____

   A. 8.05   B. 9.81   C. 12.57   D. 14.92

7. A piping sketch is drawn to a scale of 1/8" = 1 foot.   7.____
   A vertical steam line measuring 3 1/2" on the sketch would have an ACTUAL length of _____ feet.

   A. 16   B. 22   C. 24   D. 28

8. A pipe having an inside diameter of 3.48 inches and a wall thickness of .18 inches will have an outside diameter of _____ inches.   8.____

   A. 3.84   B. 3.64   C. 3.57   D. 3.51

9. A rectangular steel bar having a volume of 30 cubic inches, a width of 2 inches, and a height of 3 inches will have a length of _____ inches.   9.____

   A. 12   B. 10   C. 8   D. 5

10. A pipe weighs 20.4 pounds per foot of length.   10.____
    The total weight of eight pieces of this pipe with each piece 20 feet in length is MOST NEARLY _____ pounds.

    A. 460   B. 1,680   C. 2,420   D. 3,260

11. Assume that four pieces of pipe measuring 2'1 1/4", 4'2 3/4", 5'1 9/16", and 6'3 5/8", respectively, are cut with a saw from a pipe 20"0" long.
    Allowing 1/16" waste for each cut, the length of the remaining pipe is

    A. 2'1 9/16"   B. 2'2 9/16"   C. 2'4 13/16"   D. 2'8 9/16"

12. If one cubic inch of steel weighs 0.28 pounds, the weight, in pounds, of a steel bar 1/2" x 6" x 2'0" long is MOST NEARLY

    A. 11   B. 16   C. 20   D. 24

13. If the circumference of a circle is equal to 31.416 inches, then its diameter, in inches, is equal to MOST NEARLY

    A. 8   B. 9   C. 10   D. 13

14. Assume that a steam fitter's helper receives a salary of $171.36 a day for 250 days is considered a full work year. If taxes, social security, hospitalization, and pension deducted from his salary amounts to 16 percent of his gross pay, then his net yearly salary will be MOST NEARLY

    A. $31,788   B. $35,982   C. $41,982   D. $42,840

15. If the outside diameter of a pipe is 14 inches and the wall thickness is 1/2 inch, then the inside area of the pipe, in square inches, is MOST NEARLY

    A. 125   B. 133   C. 143   D. 154

16. A steam leak in a pipe line allows steam to escape at a rate of 50,000 pounds each month.
    Assuming that the cost of steam is $2.50 per 1,000 pounds, the TOTAL cost of wasted steam from this leak for a 12-month period would amount to

    A. $125   B. $300   C. $1,500   D. $3,000

17. If 250 feet of 4" pipe weighs 400 pounds, the weight of this pipe per linear foot is _____ pounds.

    A. 1.25   B. 1.50   C. 1.60   D. 1.75

18. A set of heating plan drawings is drawn to a scale of 1/4" = 1 foot.
    If a length of pipe measures 4 5/8" on the drawing, the ACTUAL length of the pipe, in feet, is

    A. 16.3   B. 16.8   C. 17.5   D. 18.5

19. The TOTAL length of four pieces of pipe whose lengths are 3'4 1/2", 2'1 5/16", 4'9 3/8", and 2'3 1/4", respectively, is

    A. 11'5 7/16"   B. 11'6 7/16"
    C. 12'5 7/16"   D. 12'6 7/16"

20. Assume that a pipe trench is 3 feet wide, 3 feet deep, and 300 feet long.
    If the unit cost of excavating the trench is $120 per cubic yard, the TOTAL cost of excavating the trench is

    A. $1,200   B. $12,000   C. $27,000   D. $36,000

21. The TOTAL length of four pieces of 1 1/2" galvanized steel pipe whose lengths are 7 ft. + 3 1/2 inches, 4 ft. + 2 1/4 inches, 6 ft. + 7 inches, and 8 ft. +5 1/8 inches is

   A. 26 feet + 5 7/8 inches
   B. 25 ft. + 6 7/8 inches
   C. 25 feet + 4 1/4 inches
   D. 25 ft. + 3 3/8 inches

22. A swimming pool is 25' wide by 75' long and has an average depth of 5'. 1 cubic foot contains 7.5 gallons of water. The capacity, when filled to the overflow, is _____ gallons.

   A. 9,375   B. 65,625   C. 69,005   D. 70,312

23. The sum of 3 1/4, 5 1/8, 2 1/2 , and 3 3/8 is

   A. 14   B. 14 1/8   C. 14 1/4   D. 14 3/8

24. Assume that it takes 6 men 8 days to do a particular job. If you have only 4 men available to do this job and they all work at the same speed, then the number of days it would take to complete the job would be

   A. 11   B. 12   C. 13   D. 14

25. The total length of four pieces of 2" O.D. pipe, whose lengths are 7'3 1/2", 4'2 3/16", 5'7 5/16", and 8'5 7/8", respectively, is MOST NEARLY

   A. 24'6 3/4"
   B. 24'7 15/16"
   C. 25'5 13/16"
   D. 25'6 7/8"

KEY (CORRECT ANSWERS)

1.	C		11.	B
2.	C		12.	C
3.	D		13.	C
4.	A		14.	B
5.	A		15.	B
6.	C		16.	C
7.	D		17.	C
8.	A		18.	D
9.	D		19.	D
10.	D		20.	B

21. A
22. D
23. C
24. B
25. D

SOLUTIONS TO PROBLEMS

1. 15 5/8" + 8 3/4" + 30 5/16" + 20 1/2" = 73 35/16" = 75 3/16"

2. Inside diameter = 6" - 1/2" - 1/2" = 5". Area = (π)(5/2")^2 ≈ 19.6 sq. in.

3. Pipe remaining = 14' - 1'10" - 3'2 1/2" - 5'7 1/2" - (3)(1/8") = 3'3 5/8"

4. 76.5 x 9/5 = 137.7 + 32 = 169.7

5. 7.5 x 150 = 1125

6. Radius = 2" Circumference = (2π)(2") ≈ 12.57"

7. 3 1/2" 1/8" = (7/2)(8/1) = 28 Then, (28)(1 ft.) = 28 feet

8. Outside diameter = 3.48" + .18" + .18" = 3.84"

9. 30 = (2)(3)(length). So, length = 5"

10. Total weight = (20.4)(8)(20) ≈ 3260 lbs.

11. 20' - 2'1 1/4" - 4'2 3/4" - 5'1 9/16" - 6'3 5/8" - (4)(1/16") = 2'2 9/16"

12. Weight = (.28)(1/2")(6")(24") = 20.16 ≈ 20 lbs.

13. Diameter = 31.416" ÷ π ≈ 10"

14. His net pay for 250 days = (.84)($171.36)(250) = $35,985.60 ≈ $35,928 (from answer key)

15. Inside diameter = 14" - 1/2" - 1/2" = 13". Area = (π)(13/2")^2 ≈ 133 sq.in

16. (50,000 lbs.)(12) = 600,000 lbs. per year. The cost would be ($2.50)(600) = $1500

17. 400 ÷ 250 = 1.60 pounds per linear foot

18. 4 5/8" ÷ 1/4" = 37/8 . 4/1 = 18.5 Then, (18.5)(1 ft.) = 18.5 feet

19. 3'4 1/2" + 2'1 5/16" + 4'9 3/8" + 2'3 1/4" = 11'17 23/16" = 12'6 7/16"

20. (3')(3')(300') = 2700 cu.ft., which is 2700 ÷ 27 = 100 cu.yds. Total cost = ($120)(100) = $12,000

21. 7'3 1/2" + 4'2 1/4" + 6'7" + 8'5 1/8" = 25'17 7/8" = 26'5 7/8"

22. (25)(75)(5) = 9375 cu.ft. Then, (9375)(7.5) ≈ 70,312 gals.

23. 3 1/4 + 5 1/8 + 2 1/2 + 3 3/8 = 13 10/8 = 14 1/4

24. (6)(8) = 48 man-days. Then, 48 ÷ 4 = 12 days

25. 7'3 1/2" + 4'2 3/16" + 5'7 5/16" + 8'5 7/8" = 24'17 30/16" = 25'6 7/8"

TEST 3

DIRECTIONS: Each question or incomplete statement is followed by several suggested answers or completions. Select the one that BEST answers the question or completes the statement. *PRINT THE LETTER OF THE CORRECT ANSWER IN THE SPACE AT THE RIGHT.*

1. The time required to pump 2,500 gallons of water out of a sump at the rate of 12 1/2 gallons per minutes would be _____ hour(s) _____ minutes.

   A. 1; 40   B. 2; 30   C. 3; 20   D. 6; 40

   1.____

2. Copper tubing which has an inside diameter of 1 1/16" and a wall thickness of .095" has an outside diameter which is MOST NEARLY _____ inches.

   A. 1 5/32   B. 1 3/16   C. 1 7/32   D. 1 1/4

   2.____

3. Assume that 90 gallons per minute flow through a certain 3-inch pipe which is tapped into a street main.
   The amount of water which would flow through a 1-inch pipe tapped into the same street main is MOST NEARLY _____ gpm.

   A. 90   B. 45   C. 30   D. 10

   3.____

4. The weight of a 6 foot length of 8-inch pipe which weighs 24.70 pounds per foot is _____ lbs.

   A. 148.2   B. 176.8   C. 197.6   D. 212.4

   4.____

5. If a 4-inch pipe is directly coupled to a 2-inch pipe and 16 gallons per minute are flowing through the 4-inch pipe, then the flow through the 2-inch pipe will be _____ gallons per minute.

   A. 4   B. 8   C. 16   D. 32

   5.____

6. If the water pressure at the bottom of a column of water 34 feet high is 14.7 pounds per square inch, the water pressure at the bottom of a column of water 18 feet high is MOST NEARLY _____ pounds per square inch.

   A. 8.0   B. 7.8   C. 7.6   D. 7.4

   6.____

7. If there are 7 1/2 gallons in a cubic foot of water and if water flows from a hose at a constant rate of 4 gallons per minute, the time it should take to COMPLETELY fill a tank of 1,600 cubic feet capacity with water from that hose is _____ hours.

   A. 300   B. 150   C. 100   D. 50

   7.____

8. Each of a group of fifteen water meter readers read an average of 62 water meters a day in a certain 5-day work week. A total of 5,115 meters are read by this group the following week.
   The TOTAL number of meters read in the second week as compared to the first week shows a

   A. 10% increase   B. 15% increase
   C. 20% increase   D. 5% decrease

   8.____

111

9. A certain water consumer used 5% more water in 1994 than he did in 1993. If his water consumption for 1994 was 8,375 cubic feet, the amount of water he consumed in 1993 was MOST NEARLY _____ cubic feet.

   A. 9,014   B. 8,816   C. 7,976   D. 6,776

10. Assume that a water meter reads 40,175 cubic feet and that the previous reading was 29,186 cubic feet.
    If the charge for water is 92 cents per 100 cubic feet or any fraction thereof, the bill for the amount of water used since the previous meter reading should be

    A. $100.28   B. $101.04   C. $101.08   D. $101.20

11. A leaking faucet caused a loss of 216 cubic feet of water in a 30-day month.
    If there are 7.5 gallons in a cubic foot of water, then the AVERAGE loss of water per hour for that month was _____ gallons.

    A. 2 1/4   B. 2 1/8   C. 2   D. 1 3/4

12. The fraction which is equal to .375 is

    A. 3/16   B. 5/32   C. 3/8   D. 5/12

13. A square backyard swimming pool, each side of which is 10 feet long, is filled to a depth of 3 1/2 feet.
    If there are 7 1/2 gallons in a cubic foot of water, the number of gallons of water in the pool is MOST NEARLY _____ gallons.

    A. 46.7   B. 100   C. 2,625   D. 3,500

14. When 1 5/8, 3 3/4, 6 1/3, and 9 1/2 are added, the resulting sum is

    A. 21 1/8   B. 21 1/6   C. 21 5/24   D. 21 1/4

15. When 946 1/2 is subtracted from 1,035 1/4, the result is

    A. 87 1/4   B. 87 3/4   C. 88 1/4   D. 88 3/4

16. When 39 is multiplied by 697, the result is

    A. 8,364   B. 26,283   C. 27,183   D. 28,003

17. When 16.074 is divided by .045, the result is

    A. 3.6   B. 35.7   C. 357.2   D. 3,572

18. To dig a trench 3'0" wide, 50'0" long, and 5'6" deep, the total number of cubic yards of earth to be removed is MOST NEARLY

    A. 30   B. 90   C. 140   D. 825

19. The TOTAL length of four pieces of 2" pipe, whose lengths are 7'3 1/2", 4'2 3/16", 5'7 5/16", and 8'5 7/8", respectively, is

    A. 24'6 3/4"   B. 24'7 15/16"
    C. 25'5 13/16"   D. 25'6 7/8"

20. A hot water line made of copper has a straight horizontal run of 150 feet and, when installed, is at a temperature of 45° F. In use, its temperature rises to 190° F.
    If the coefficient of expansion for copper is 0.0000095" per foot per degree F, the TOTAL expansion, in inches, in the run of pipe is given by the product of 150 multiplied by 0.0000095 by

    A. 145
    B. 145 x 12
    C. 145 divided by 12
    D. 145 x 12 x 12

21. A water storage tank measures 5' long, 4' wide, and 6' deep and is filled to the 5 1/2' mark with water.
    If one cubic foot of water weighs 62 pounds, the number of pounds of water required to COMPLETELY fill the tank is

    A. 7,440
    B. 6,200
    C. 1,240
    D. 620

22. Assume that a pipe worker earns $83,125.00 per year.
    If seventeen percent of his pay is deducted for taxes, social security, and pension, his net weekly pay will be APPROXIMATELY

    A. $1598.50
    B. $1504.00
    C. $1453.00
    D. $1325.00

23. If eighteen feet of 4" cast iron pipe weighs approximately 390 pounds, the weight of this pipe per lineal foot will be MOST NEARLY _____ lbs.

    A. 19
    B. 22
    C. 23
    D. 25

24. If it takes 3 men 11 days to dig a trench, the number of days it will take 5 men to dig the same trench, assuming all work is done at the same rate of speed, is MOST NEARLY

    A. 6 1/2
    B. 7 3/4
    C. 8 1/4
    D. 8 3/4

25. If a trench is dug 6'0" deep, 2'6" wide, and 8'0" long, the area of the opening, in square feet, is MOST NEARLY

    A. 48
    B. 32
    C. 20
    D. 15

KEY (CORRECT ANSWERS)

1. C
2. D
3. D
4. A
5. B

6. B
7. D
8. A
9. C
10. D

11. A
12. C
13. C
14. C
15. D

16. C
17. C
18. A
19. D
20. A

21. D
22. D
23. B
24. A
25. C

SOLUTIONS TO PROBLEMS

1. 2500 ÷ 12 1/2 = 200 min. = 3 hrs. 20 min.

2. 1 1/16" + .095" + .095" = 1.0625 + .095 + .095 = 1.2525" ≈ 1 1/4"

3. Cross-sectional areas for a 3-inch pipe and a 1-inch pipe are $(\pi)(1.5)^2$ and $(\pi)(.5)^2$ = 2.25π and .25π, respectively. Let x = amount of water flowing through the 1-inch pipe. Then, $\frac{90}{x} = \frac{2.25\pi}{.25\pi}$. Solving, x = 10 gals/min

4. (24.70)(6) = 148.2 lbs.

5. $\frac{4" \text{ pipe}}{16 \text{ gallons}} = \frac{2" \text{ pipe}}{x \text{ gallons}}$, 4x = 32, x = 8

6. Let x = pressure. Then, 34/18 = 14.7/x. Solving, x ≈ 7.8

7. (1600)(7.5) = 12,000 gallons. Then, 12,000 ÷ 4 = 3000 min. = 50 hours

8. (15)(62)(5) = 4650. Then, (5115-4650)/4650 = 10% increase

9. 8375 ÷ 1.05 ≈ 7976 cu.ft.

10. 40,175 - 29,186 = 10,989 cu.ft. Then, 10,989 100 = 109.89. Since .92 is charged for each 100 cu.ft. or fraction thereof, total cost = (.92)(110) = $101.20

11. (216)(7.5) = 1620 gallons. In 30 days, there are 720 hours. Thus, the average water loss per hour = 1620 ÷ 720 = 2 1/4 gallons.

12. .375 = 375/1000 = 3/8

13. Volume = (10)(10)(3 1/2) = 350 cu.ft. Then, (350)(7 1/2) = 2625 gallons

14. 1 5/8 + 3 3/4 + 6 1/3 + 9 1/2 = 19 53/24 = 21 5/24

15. 1035 1/4 - 946 1/2 = 88 3/4

16. (39)(697) = 27,183

17. 16.074 .045 = 357.2

18. (3')(50')(5 1/2') = 825 cu.ft. ≈ 30 cu.yds., since 1 cu.yd. = 27 cu.ft.

19. 7'3 1/2" + 4'2 3/16" + 5'7 5/16" + 8'5 7/8" = 24'17 30/16" = 25'6 7/8"

20. Total expansion = (150)(.0000095)(145)

21. Number of pounds needed = (5)(4)(6-5 1/2)(62) = 620

22. Net annual pay = ($83,125)(.83) ≈ $69000. Then, the net weekly pay = $69000 ÷ 52 ≈ $1325 (actually about $1327)

23. 390 lbs. ÷ 18 = 21.6 lbs. per linear foot

24. (3)(11) = 33 man-days. Then, 33 ÷ 5 = 6.6 ≈ 6 1/2 days

25. Area = (8')(2 1/2') = 20 sq.ft.

HEATING AND ENVIRONMENTAL CONTROL

CONTENTS

		Page
I.	Introduction	1
II.	Definitions	1
III.	Fuels	3
IV.	Central Heating Units	6
V.	Fuel-Burning Procedures and Automatic Firing Equipment	9
VI.	Refractory	11
VII.	Heating Systems	11
VIII.	Domestic Hot Water Jack Stoves (Coal Stoves)	23
IX.	Hazardous Installations	23

HEATING AND ENVIRONMENTAL CONTROL

I. Introduction

The function of a heating system is to provide for human comfort. The variables to be controlled are temperature, air motion, and relative humidity. Temperature must be maintained uniformly throughout the heated area. Field experience indicates a variation from 6 to 10 degrees F from floor to ceiling. The adequacy of the heating device and the tightness of the structure or room determine the degree of personal comfort within the dwelling.

Coal, wood, oil, gas, and electricity are the main sources of heat energy. Heating systems commonly used are steam, hot water, and hot air. The housing inspector should have a knowledge of the various heating fuels and systems to be able to determine their adequacy and safety in operation. To cover fully all aspects of the heating system, the entire area and physical components of the system must be considered.

II. Definitions

A **Anti-flooding Control** — A safety control that shuts off fuel and ignition when excessive fuel accumulates in the appliance.

B **Appliance:**
   1 **High-heat** — a unit that operates with flue entrance temperature of combustion products above 1,500°F.
   2 **Medium heat** — same as high-heat, except above 600°F.
   3 **Low heat** — same as high heat, except below 600°F.

C **Boiler:**
   1 **High pressure** – a boiler furnishing pressure at 15 psi or more.
   2 **Low pressure** — (hot water or steam) — a boiler furnishing steam at a pressure less than 15 psi or hot water not more than 30 psi.

D **Burner** — A device that provides the mixing of fuel, air, and ignition in a combustion chamber.

E **Chimney** — A vertical shaft containing one or more passageways.
   1 **Factory-built chimney** — a tested and accredited flue for venting gas appliances, incinerators and solid or liquid fuel-burning appliances.
   2 **Masonry chimney** — a field-constructed chimney built of masonry and lined with terra cotta flue or firebrick.
   3 **Metal chimney** — a field-constructed chimney of metal.
   4 **Chimney Connector** — A pipe or breeching that connects the heating appliance to the chimney.

F **Clearance** — The distance separating the appliance, chimney connector, plenum, and flue from the nearest surface of combustible material.

G **Central Heating System** — A boiler or furnace, flue connected, installed as an integral part of the structure and designed to supply heat adequately for the structure.

H **Controls:**
   1 **High-low limit control** — an automatic control that responds to liquid level changes and pressure or temperature changes and that limits operation of the appliance to be controlled.

2 **Primary safety control** — the automatic safety control intended to prevent abnormal discharge of fuel at the burner in case of ignition failure or flame failure.

3 **Combustion safety control** — a primary safety control that responds to flame properties, sensing the presence of flame and causing fuel to be shut off in event of flame failure.

I **Convector** — A convector is a radiator that supplies a maximum amount of heat by convection, using many closely-spaced metal fins fitted onto pipes that carry hot water or steam and thereby heat the circulating air.

J **Conversion** — a boiler or furnace, flue connected, originally designed for solid fuel but converted for liquid or gas fuel.

K **Damper** — a valve for regulating draft. Generally located on the exhaust side of the combustion chamber, usually in the chimney connector.

L **Draft Hood** — a device placed in and made a part of the vent connector (chimney connector or smoke pipe) from an appliance, or in the appliance itself, that is designed to (a) ensure the ready escape of the products of combustion in the event of no draft, back-draft, or stoppage beyond the draft hood; (b) prevent backdraft from entering the appliance; (c) neutralize the effect of stack action of the chimney flue upon appliance operation.

M **Draft Regulator** — a device that functions to maintain a desired draft in oil-fired appliances by automatically reducing the chimney draft to the desired value. Sometimes this device is referred to, in the field, as air-balance, air-stat, or flue velocity control.

N **Fuel Oil** — a liquid mixture or compound derived from petroleum that does not emit flammable vapor below a temperature of 125°F.

O **Heat** — the warming of a building, apartment, or room by a stove, furnace, or electricity.

P **Heating Plant** — the furnace, boiler, or the other heating devices used to generate steam, hot water, or hot air, which then is circulated through a distribution system. It uses coal, gas, oil, or wood as its source of heat.

Q **Limit Control** — a thermostatic device installed in the duct system to shut off the supply of heat at a predetermined temperature of the circulated air.

R **Oil Burner** — a device for burning oil in heating appliances such as boilers, furnaces, water heaters, and ranges. A burner of this type may be a pressure-atomizing gun type, a horizontal or vertical rotary type, or a mechanical or natural draft-vaporizing type.

S **Oil Stove** — a flue-connected, self-contained, self-supporting oil-burning range or room heater equipped with an integral tank not exceeding 10 gallons; it may be designed to be connected to a separate oil supply tank.

T **Plenum Chamber** — an air compartment to which one or more distributing air ducts are connected.

U **Pump, Automatic Oil** — a device that automatically pumps oil from the supply tank and delivers it in specific quantities to an oil-burning appliance. The pump or device is designed to stop pumping automatically in case of a breakage of the oil supply line.

V **Radiant Heat** — a method of heating a building by means of electric coils, hot water, or steam pipes installed in the floors, walls, or ceilings.

W **Register** — a grille-covered opening in a floor or wall through which hot or cold air can be introduced into a room. It may or may not be arranged to permit closing of the grille.

X **Room Heater** — a self-contained, free-standing heating appliance intended for installation in the space being heated and not intended for duct connection (space heater).

Y **Smoke Detector** — a device installed in the plenum chamber or in the main supply air duct of an air-conditioning system to shut off the blower automatically and close a fire damper in the presence of smoke.

Z **Tank** — a separate tank connected, directly or by pump, to an oil-burning appliance.

AA **Thimble** — a term applied to a metal or terra cotta lining for a chimney or furnace pipe.

BB **Valve — Main Shut-off Valve** — a manually operated valve in an oil line for the purpose of turning on or off the oil supply to the burner.

CC **Vent System** — the gas vent or chimney and vent connector, if used, assembled to form a continuous, unobstructed passageway from the gas appliance to the outside atmosphere for the purpose of removing vent gases.

III. Fuels

A Coal

Classification and composition — the four types of coal are: anthracite, bituminous, sub-bituminous, and lignitic.

Coal is prepared in many sizes and combinations of sizes. The combustible portions of the coal are fixed carbons, volatile matter (hydrocarbons), and small amounts of sulfur. In combination with these are non-combustible elements composed of moisture and impurities that form ash. The various types differ in heat content. The heat content is determined by analysis and is expressed in British Thermal Units (BTU) per pound. The type and size of coal used are determined by the availability and by the equipment in which it is burned.

The type and size of coal must be proper for the particular heating unit; that is, the furnace grate and flue size must be designed for the particular type of coal. Excessive coal gas can be generated through improper firing as a result of improper fuel or improper furnace design, or both.

The owner should be questioned about his procedure for adding coal to his furnace. It should be explained that a period of time must be allowed to pass before damping to prevent the release of excessive coal gas. This should also be done before damping for the night or other periods when full draft is not required.

Improper coal furnace operation can result in an extremely hazardous and unhealthful occupancy — the inspector should be able to offer helpful operational procedures. Ventilation of the area surrounding the furnace is very important in order to prevent heat buildup and to supply air for combustion.

B Fuel Oil

Fuel oils are derived from petroleum, which consists primarily of compounds of hydrogen and carbon (hydrocarbons) and smaller amounts of nitrogen and sulfur.

Classification of fuel oils Domestic fuel oils are controlled by rigid specifications. Six grades of fuel oil are generally used in heating systems; the lighter two grades are used primarily for domestic heating.

These grades are:

1. **Grade Number 1** — A volatile, distillate oil for use in burners that prepare fuel for burning solely by vaporization (oil-fired space heaters).

2. **Grade Number 2** — A moderate-weight, volatile, distillate oil used for burners that prepare oil for burning by a combination of vaporization and atomization. This grade of oil is commonly used in domestic heating furnaces.

3. **Grade Number 3** — A low-viscosity, distillate oil used in burners wherein fuel and air are prepared for burning solely by atomization.

4. **Grade Number 4** — A medium-viscosity oil used in burners without preheating. (Small industrial or apartment house applications.)

5. **Grade Number 5** — A medium-viscosity oil used in burners with preheaters that require an oil of lower viscosity than Grade Number 6. (Industrial or apartment house application.)

6. **Grade Number 6** — A high-viscosity oil for use in burners with preheating facilities adequate for handling oil of high viscosity. (Industrial applications.)

7. **Heat content** — Heating values of oil vary from approximately 152,000 BTU per gallon for Number 6 oil to 136,000 BTU per gallon for Number 1.

Oil is more widely used today than coal and provides a more automatic source of heat and comfort. It also requires more complicated systems and controls.

If the oil supply is used within the basement or cellar area, certain basic regulations must be followed (see Figure 1). No more than two 275-gallon tanks may be installed above ground in the lowest story of any one building. The tank shall not be closer than 7 feet horizontally to any boiler, furnace, stove, or exposed flame. Fuel oil lines should be embedded in a concrete or cement floor or protected against damage if they run across the floor. Bach tank must have a shutoff valve that will stop the flow from each tank if a leak develops in the line to or in the burner itself.

The tank or tanks must be vented to the outside, and a gauge showing the quantity of oil in the tank or tanks must be tight and operative. Tanks must be off the floor and on a stable base to prevent settlement or movement that may rupture the connections.

A buried outside tank installation is shown in Figure 2.

C Gas

Commercial gas fuels are colorless gases. Some have a characteristic pungent odor, while others are odorless and cannot be detected by smell. Although gas fuels are easily handled in heating equipment, their presence in air in appreciable quantities becomes a serious health hazard. Gases diffuse readily in the air, making explosive mixtures possible. (A proportion of combustible gas and air that is ignited burns with such a high velocity that an explosive force is created.) Because of these characteristics of gas fuels, precautions must be taken to prevent leaks, and care must be exercised when gas-fired equipment is lit.

Classification of gas - Gas is broadly classified as natural or manufactured.

1. **Manufactured Gas** — This gas as distributed is usually a combination of certain proportions of gases produced by two or more processes as obtained from coke, coal, and petroleum. Its BTU value per cubic foot is generally closely regulated, and costs are determined on a guaran-

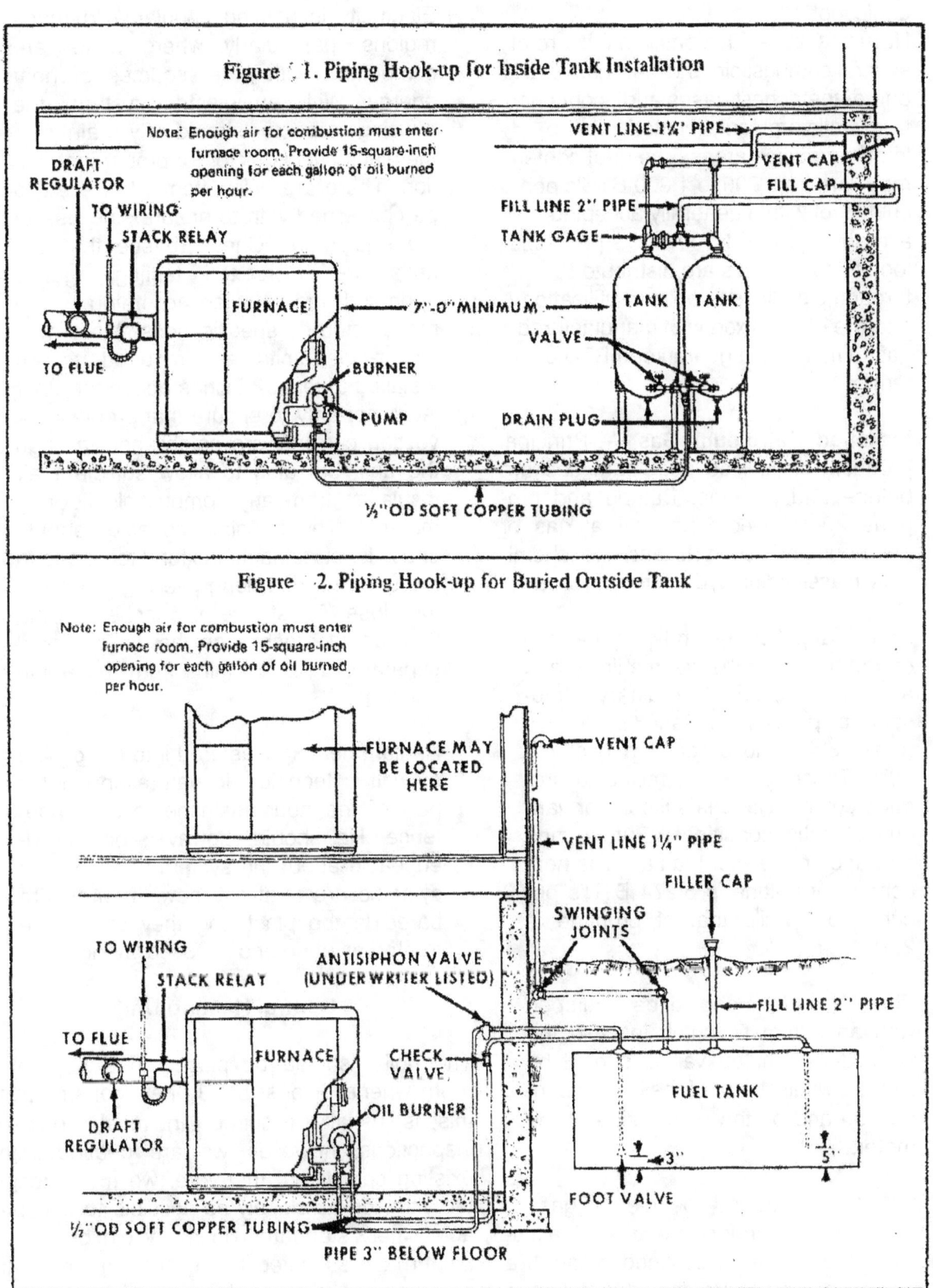

teed BTU basis, usually 520 to 540 per cubic foot.

2. **Natural Gas** — This gas is a mixture of several combustible and inert gases. It is one of the richest gases and is obtained from wells ordinarily located in petroleum-producing areas. The heat content may vary from 700 to 1,300 BTU's per cubic foot with a generally accepted average figure of 1,000 BTU's per cubic foot. Natural gases are distributed through pipe lines to point of utilization and are often mixed with manufactured gas to maintain a guaranteed BTU content.

3. **Liquified Petroleum Gas** — Principal products of liquified petroleum gas are butane and propane. Butane and propane are derived from natural gas or petroleum refinery gas and are chemically classified as hydrocarbon gases.

Specifically, butane and propane are on the borderline between a liquid and a gaseous state. At ordinary atmospheric pressure butane is a gas above 33°F and propane a gas at -42°F. These gases are mixed to produce commercial gas suitable for various climatic conditions. Butane and propane are heavier than air. The heat content of butane is 3,274 BTU's per cubic foot while that of propane is 2,519.

The gas burner should be equipped with an automatic cutoff in case the flame fails. Shutoff valves should be located within 1 foot of the burner connection and on the output side of the meter.

CAUTION — Liquified petroleum gas is heavier than air; therefore, the gas will accumulate at the bottom of confined areas. If a leak should develop, care should be taken to ventilate the appliance before lighting.

D Electricity

Electricity is gaining popularity in many regions, particularly where costs are competitive with other sources of heat energy. With an electric system, the housing inspector should rely mainly on the electrical inspector for proper installation. There are a few items, however, to be concerned with to ensure safe use of the equipment. Check to see that the units are accredited testing agency approved and installed according to the manufacturer's specifications. Most convector-type units are required to be installed at least 2 inches above the floor level, not only to ensure that proper convection currents are established through the unit, but also to allow sufficient air insulation from any combustible flooring material. The housing inspector should check for curtains that extend too close to the unit or loose, long pile rugs that are too close. A distance of 6 inches on the floor and 12 inches on the walls should separate rug or curtains from the appliance.

Radiant heating plastered into the ceiling or wall is technical in nature and not a part of the housing inspector's competence. He should, however, be knowledgeable about the system used. These systems are relatively new. If wires are bared in the plastering they should be treated as open and exposed wiring.

IV. Central Heating Units

The boiler should be placed in a separate room whenever possible; in new construction this is usually required. In most housing inspections, however, we are dealing with existing conditions; therefore, we must adapt the situation as closely as possible to acceptable safety standards. In many old buildings the furnace is located in the center of the cellar or basement, and this location does not lend itself for practical conversion to a boiler room.

A Boiler Location

Consider the physical requirements for a boiler room.

1. Ventilation — More circulating air is required for the boiler room than for a habitable room, in order to reduce the heat buildup caused by the boiler or furnace as well as to supply oxygen for combustion.

2. Fire Protection Rating — As specified by various codes (fire code, building code, and insurance underwriters) the fire regulations must be strictly adhered to in areas surrounding the boiler or furnace. This minimum dimension from which a boiler or furnace is to be spaced from a wall or ceiling is shown in Figure 3.

Many times the enclosure of the furnace or boiler creates a problem of providing adequate air supply and ventilation for the room. Where codes and local authority permit, it may be more practical to place the furnace or boiler in an open area. The ceiling above the furnace should be fire protected to a distance of 3 feet beyond all furnace or boiler appurtenances and this area should be free of all storage material. The furnace or boiler should be set on a firm foundation of concrete if located in the cellar or basement. If the codes permit furnace installations on the first floor, then the building code must be consulted for proper setting and location.

B Heating Boilers

Boilers may be classified according to several kinds of characteristics. The material may be cast iron or steel. Their construction may be section, portable, fire-tube, water-tube, or special. Domestic heating boilers are generally of low-pressure type with a maximum working pressure of 15 pounds per square inch for steam and 30 pounds per square inch for hot water.

All boilers have a combustion chamber for burning fuel. Automatic fuel-firing devices help supply the fuel and control the combustion. Handfiring is accomplished by the provision of a grate, ash pit, and controllable drafts to admit air under the fuel bed and over it through slots in the firing door. A check draft is required at the smoke pipe connection to control chimney draft. The gas passes from the combustion chamber to the flue, passages (smoke pipe) designed for maximum possible transfer of heat from the gas. Provisions must be made for cleaning flue passages.

The term boiler is applied to the single heat source that can supply either steam or hot-water (boiler is often called a heater).

Cast iron boilers are generally classified as:
1. Square or rectangular boilers with vertical sections.
2. Round, square, or rectangular boilers with horizontal pancake sections.

Cast iron boilers are usually shipped in sections and assembled at the site.

C Steel Boilers

Most steel boilers are assembled units with welded steel construction and are called portable boilers. Larger boilers are installed in refractory brick settings built on the site. Above the combustion chamber a group of tubes is suspended, usually horizontally, between two headers. If flue gases pass through the tubes and water surrounds them, the boiler is designated as the fire-tube type. When water flows through the tubes, it is termed water-tube. Fire-tube is the predominant type.

D Heating Furnaces

Heating furnaces are the heat sources used when air is the heat-carrying medium. When air circulates because of the different densities of the heated and cooled air, the furnace is a gravity type. A fan may be included for the air circulation; this type is called a mechanical warm-air furnace. Furnaces may be of cast iron or steel and burn various types of fuel.

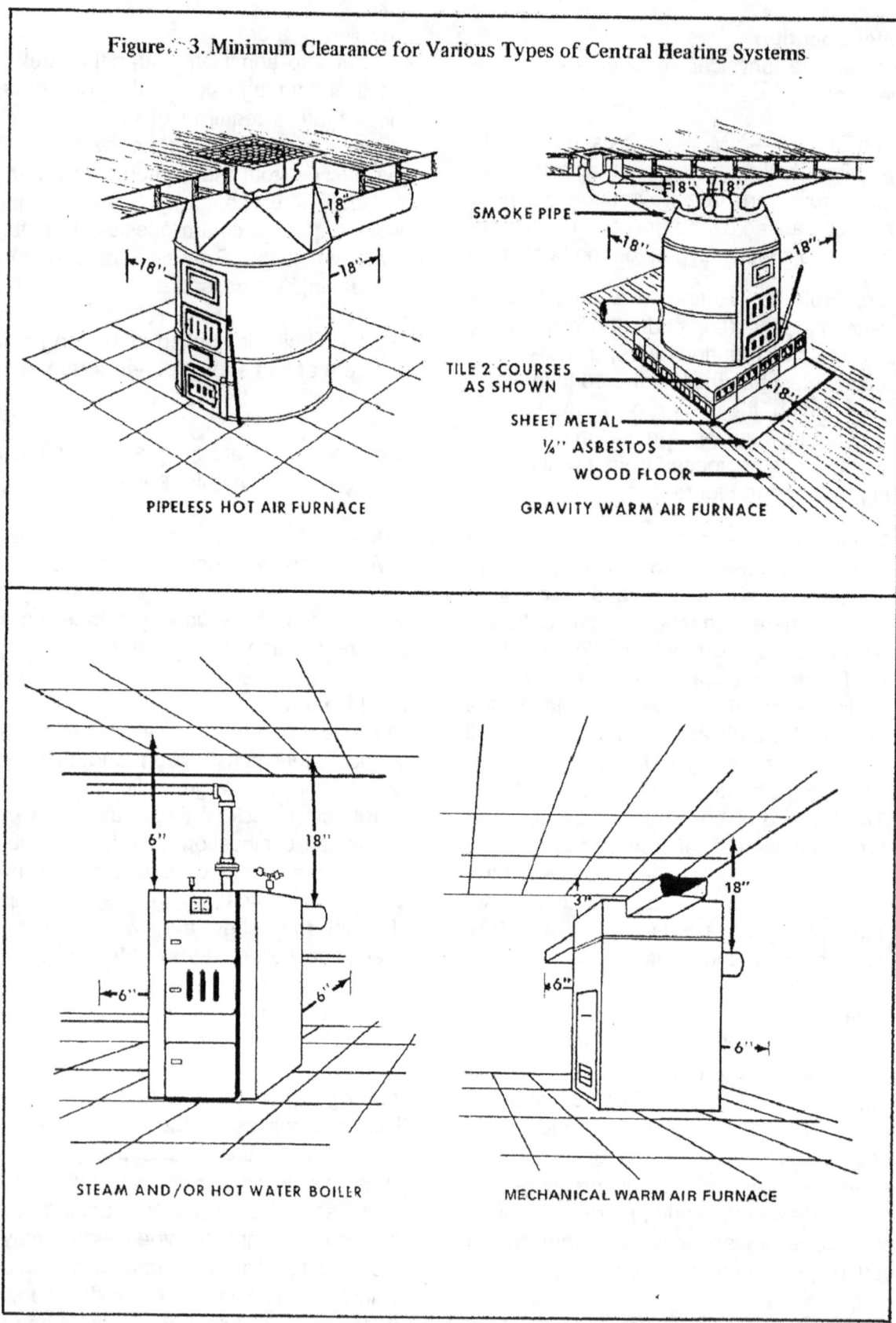

Figure 3. Minimum Clearance for Various Types of Central Heating Systems

V. Fuel-Burning Procedures and Automatic Firing Equipment

A Coal — Many localities throughout the nation still use coal as a heating fuel.

1. **Hand Stoking** - In many older furnaces, the coal is stoked or fed into the fire box by hand.

2. **Automatic Stokers** - The single-retort, underfeed-type bituminous coal stoker is the most commonly used domestic-type steam or hot water boiler (see Figure 4). The stoker consists of a coal hopper, a screw for conveying coal from hopper to retort, a fan that supplies air for combustion, a transmission for driving coalfeed and fan, and an electric motor for supplying power. The air for combustion is admitted to the fuel through tuyeres at the top of the retort. The stoker feeds coal to the furnace intermittently in accordance with the temperature or pressure demands.

B Oil Burners — Oil burners are broadly designated as distillate, domestic, and commercial or industrial. Distillate burners are usually found in oil-fired space heaters. Domestic oil burners are usually power driven and are used in domestic heating plants. Commercial or industrial burners are used in larger central-heating plants for steam or power generation.

1. **Domestic Oil Burners** — These vaporize and atomize the oil, and deliver a predetermined quantity of oil and air to the combustion chambers. Domestic oil burners operate automatically to maintain a desired temperature.

    a. **Gun-type burners** — These burners atomize the oil either by oil pressure or by low-pressure air forced through a nozzle.

The oil system pressure atomizing burner (see Figure 5) consists of a strainer, pump, pressure-regulating valve, shutoff valve, and atomizing nozzle. The air system consists of a power-drive fan and an air tube that surrounds the nozzle and electrode assembly. The fan and oil pump are generally connected directly to the motor. Oil pressures normally used are about 100 pounds per square inch, but pressures con-

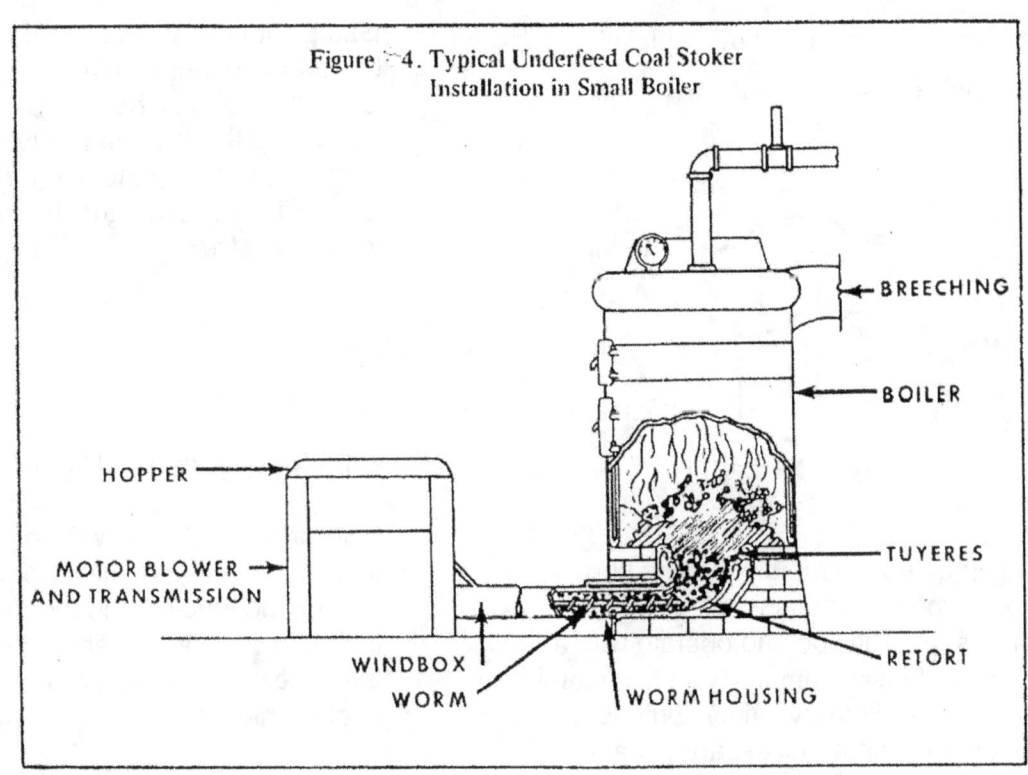

Figure 4. Typical Underfeed Coal Stoker Installation in Small Boiler

siderably in excess of this are sometimes used.

The form and parts of low-pressure air-atomizing burners (see Figure 5), are similar to high-pressure atomizing burners except for addition of a small air pump, and a different way of delivering air and oil to the nozzle or orifice.

b **Vertical rotary burners** - The atomizing-type burner, sometimes known as a radiant or suspended-flame burner, atomizes oil by throwing it from the circumference of a rapidly rotating motor-driven cup. The burner is installed so that the driving parts are protected from the heat of the flame by a hearth of refractory material at about the grate elevation. Oil is fed by pump or gravity, while the draft is mechanical or a combination of natural and mechanical.

c **Horizontal rotary burners** These were originally designed for commercial and industrial use but are available in sizes suitable for domestic use. In this burner, oil is atomized by being thrown in a

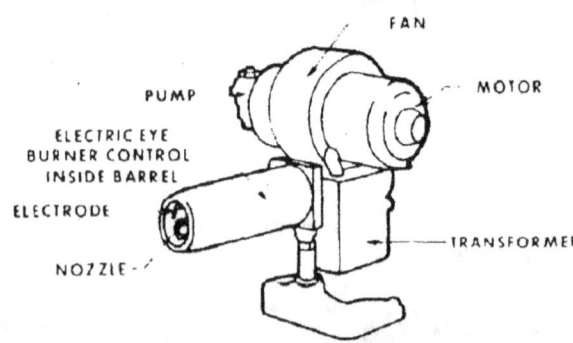

Figure 5. Cut-Away of Typical High-Pressure Gun-Burner

conical spray from a rapidly rotating cup. Horizontal rotary burners employ electric-gas or gas-pilot ignition and operate with a wide range of fuels, primarily with Numbers 1 and 2 fuel oil. Primary safety controls for burner operation are. necessary. An anti-flooding device must be a part of the system so that, if ignition in the burner should fail, the oil will not continue to flow. Likewise, a stack control is necessary to shut off the burner if the stack temperatures become excessive. A reset button on the older stack control units releases if excessive (predetermined) temperatures are exceeded and thus cuts off all power to the burner. This button must be reset before starting can be attempted. The newer models now use electric eye-type control on the burner itself.

2 **Ignition** — On the basis of the method employed to ignite fuels, burners are divided into five groups as follows:

a **Electric** — A high-voltage electric spark is made in the path of an oil and air mixture and this causes ignition. This electric spark may be continuous or may be in operation only long enough to ignite the oil. Electric ignition is almost universally used. Electrodes are located near the nozzles (see Figure 5) but not in the path of the oil spray.

b **Gas pilot** — A small gas pilot light that burns continuously is frequently used. Gas pilots usually have expanding gas valves that automatically increase flame size when motor circuit starts. After a fixed interval, the flame reverts to normal size.

c. **Electric gas** — An electric spark ignites a gas jet, which in turn ignites the oil air mixture.

d **Oil pilot** — A small oil flame is used.

e **Manual** — A burning wick or torch is placed in the combustion space through peepholes and thus ignites the charge. Operator should stand to one side of the fire door to guard against injury from chance explosion.

VI. Refractory

The refractory lining or material should be an insulating fireproof brick-like substance. Never use ordinary firebrick. The insulating brick should be set on end so as to build a 2 inch-thick wall in the pot. Size and shape of the refractory pot vary from furnace to furnace (see Figure 6 for various shapes). The shape can be either round or square, whichever is more convenient to build. It is important to use a special cement having properties similar to that of the insulating refractory-type brick.

VII. Heating Systems

A Steam Heating Systems - Steam heating systems are classified according to the pipe arrangement, accessories used, method of returning the con-densate to the boiler, method of expelling air from the system, or the type of control employed. The successful operation of a steam heating system consists of generating steam in sufficient quantity to equalize building heat loss at maximum efficiency, expelling entrapped air, and returning all condensate to the boiler rapidly. Steam cannot enter a space filled with air or water at pressure equal to the steam pressure. It is important, therefore, to eliminate air and to remove water from the distribution system. All hot pipe lines exposed to contact by residents must be properly insulated or guarded.

Steam heating systems are classified according to the method of returning the condensate to the boiler.

1 Gravity One-pipe Air-vent System — The gravity one-pipe air-vent system is one of the earliest types used. The condensate is returned to the boiler by gravity. This system is generally found in one-building-type heating systems. The steam is supplied by the boiler and carried through a single system or pipe to radiators as shown in Figure 7. Return of the condensate is dependent on hydrostatic head. Therefore, the end of the steam main, where it attaches to the boiler, must be full of water (termed a wet return) for a distance above the boiler line to create a pressure drop balance between the boiler and the steam main.

Radiators are equipped with an inlet valve and with an air valve (see Figure 8). The air valve permits venting of air from the radiator and its displacement by steam. Condensate is drained from the radiator through the same pipe that supplies steam.

2 Two-pipe Steam Vapor System with Return Trap — The two-pipe vapor system with boiler return trap and air eliminator is an improvement of the one-pipe system. The return connection of the radiator has a thermostatic trap that permits flow of condensate and air only from the radiator and prevents steam from leaving the radiator. Since the return main is at atmospheric pressure or less, a boiler return trap is installed to equalize condensate return pressure with boiler pressure.

B **Hot Water Heating Systems** — All hot water heating systems are similar in design and operating principle.

1 One-pipe Gravity System — The one-pipe gravity hot water heating system is the most elementary of the gravity systems and is shown in Figure 9. Water is heated at the lowest point in the system. It rises through a single main because of a difference in density between hot and cold water. The supply rise or radiator branch takes off from the top of the main to supply water to the radiators. After the water gives up heat in the radiator it goes back to the same main through return piping from the radiator. This cooler return water mixes with water in the supply main and causes the water to cool a little. As a result, the next radiator on the system has a lower emission rate and must be larger.

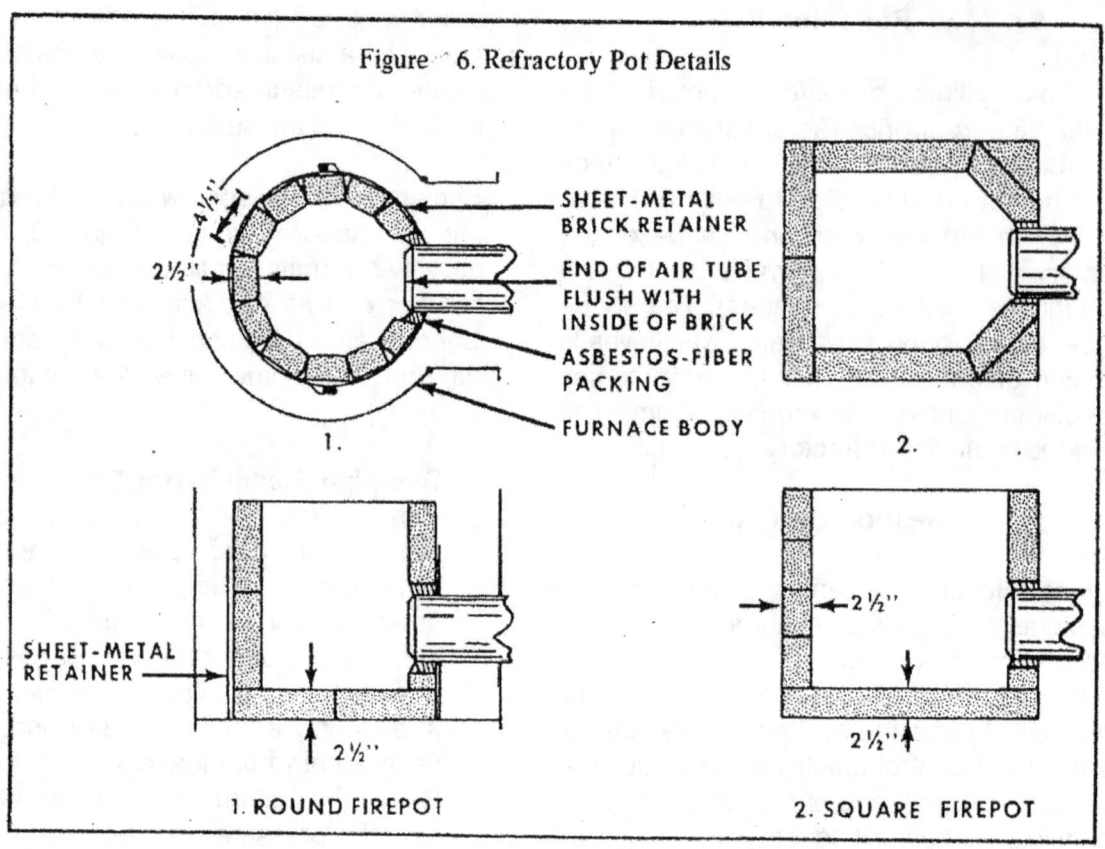

Figure 6. Refractory Pot Details

1. ROUND FIREPOT
2. SQUARE FIREPOT

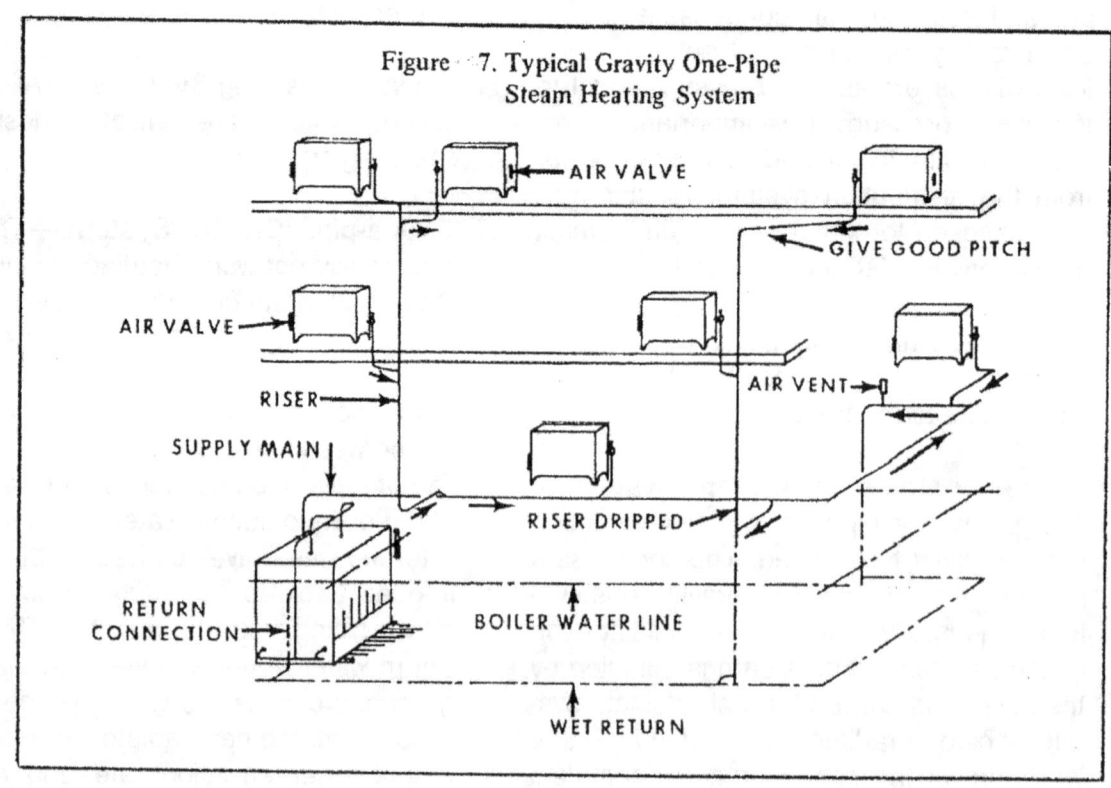

Figure 7. Typical Gravity One-Pipe Steam Heating System

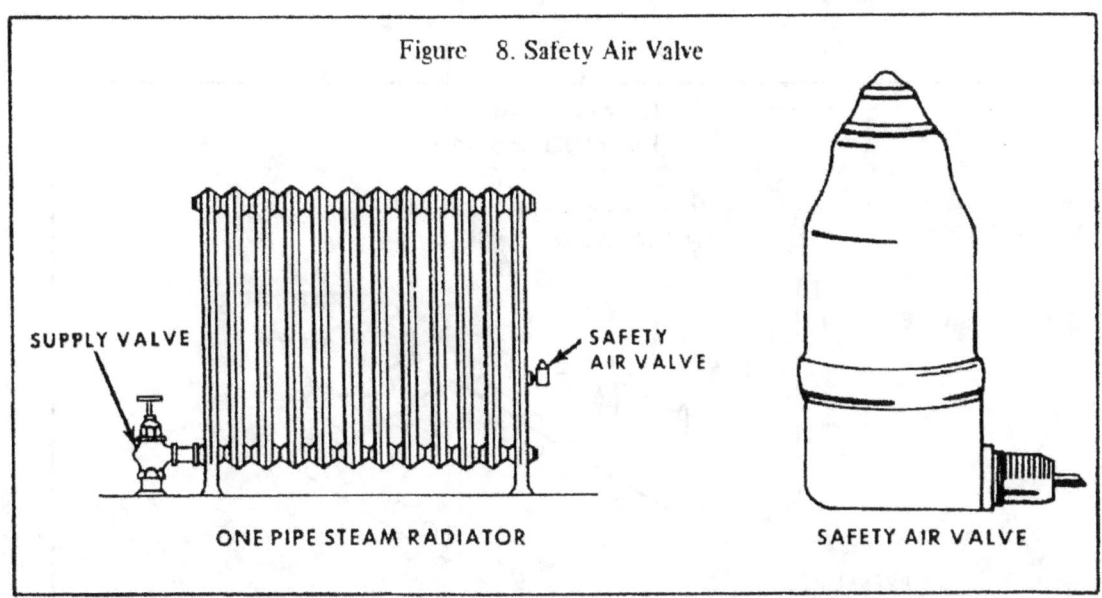

Figure 8. Safety Air Valve

Note in Figure 9 that the high points of the hot water system are vented and the low points are drained. In this case, the radiators are the high points and the heater is the low point.

2 **One-pipe Forced-feed System** — If a pump or circulator is introduced in the main near the heater of the one-pipe system, we have a forced system that can be used for much larger applications than the gravity type. This system can operate at higher water temperatures than the gravity system. The faster moving higher temperature water makes a more responsive system with a smaller temperature drop through each radiator. Higher operating temperatures and lower temperature drops permit the use of smaller radiators for the same heating load.

3 **Two-pipe Gravity Systems** — One-pipe gravity systems may become a two-pipe system if the return radiator branch connects to a second main that returns water to the heater (see Figure 10). Water temperature is practically the same in all the radiators.

4 **Two-pipe Forced-circulation System** — This system is similar to a one-pipe forced-circulation system except that the same piping arrangement is found in the two-pipe gravity flow system.

5 **Expansion Tanks** — When water is heated it tends to expand. Therefore, in a hot water system an expansion tank is necessary. The expansion tank, either of open or closed type, must be of sufficient size to permit a change in water volume within the heating system. If the expansion tank is of the open type it must be placed at least 3 feet above the highest point of the system. It will require a vent and an overflow. The open tank is usually in an attic, where it needs protection from freezing.

The enclosed expansion tank is found in modern installations. An air cushion in the tank compresses and expands according to the change of volume and pressure in the system. Closed tanks are usually at the low point in the system and close to the heater. They can, however, be placed at almost any location within the heating system.

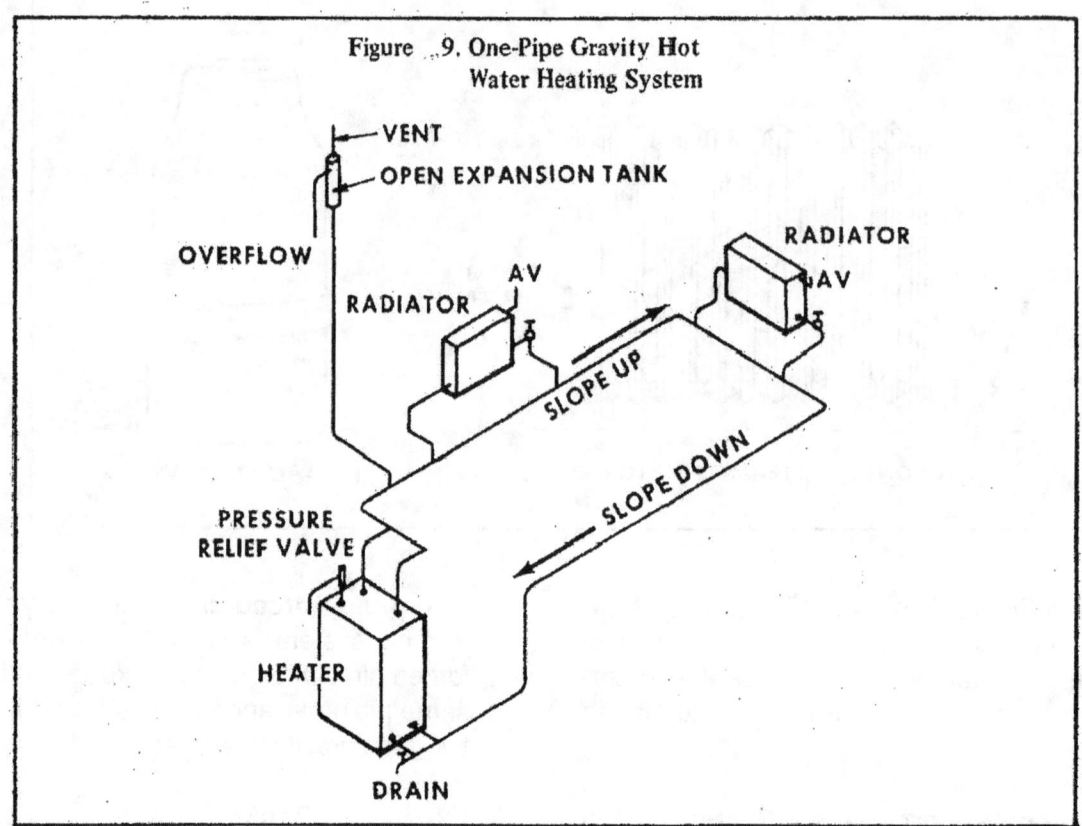

Figure 9. One-Pipe Gravity Hot Water Heating System

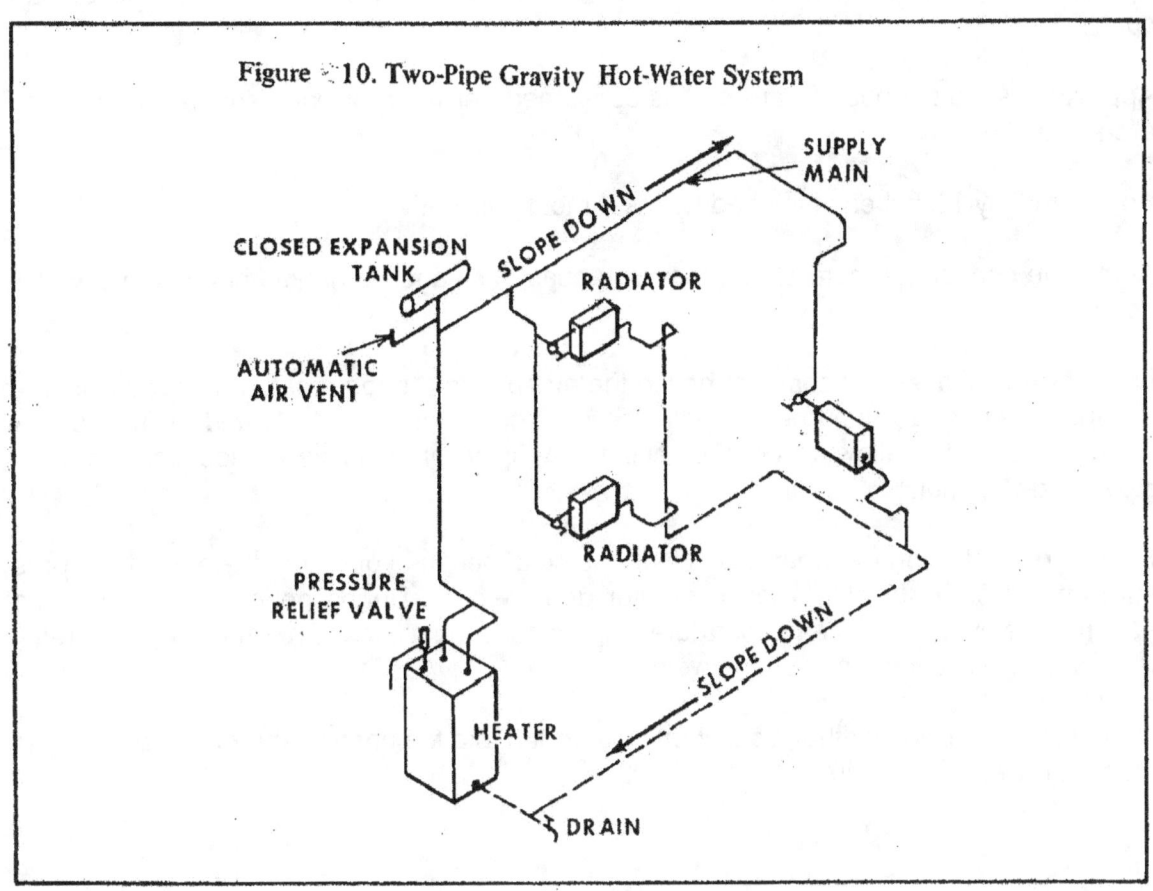

Figure 10. Two-Pipe Gravity Hot-Water System

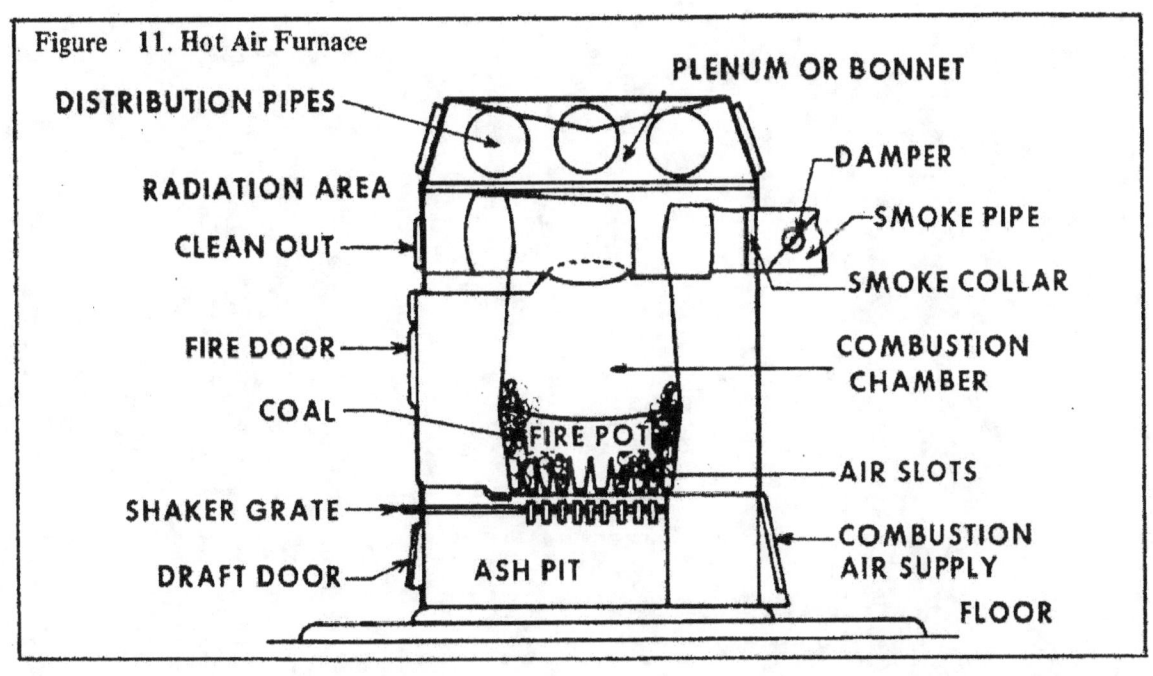

Figure 11. Hot Air Furnace

COAL NOTES

1. Approximately 12 pounds of air is required for complete combustion of 1 pound of hard coal.

2. Approximately 5 pounds of hard coal is consumed per hour for each square foot of grate area.

3. Approximately 12 inches of fire bed will heat most efficiently.

4. Anthracite coal burns more slowly than soft coal, is cleaner to handle-hence more widely used.

5. Large-size coal does not compact-hence the air spaces are too great and allows gases to escape into the flue unburned. Small size coal compacts too much and inhibits airflow through the coal to allow for good combustion. Mixing of coal size is recommended, i.e., stove and chestnut.

6. Fires burn best when the weather is clear and cold, because of reduced atmospheric pressure on the air in the flue—hence greater draft velocity. During periods of heavy atmosphere or rainy weather the temperature of flue gases must exceed normal temperatures to overcome the heavier atmospheric weight.

7. During extreme cold weather, coal should be added to a fire once in approximately 8 hours; moderate weather-12 hours.

C Hot Air Heating Systems

1 Gravity-Warm-Air Heating Systems —
These operate because of the difference in specific gravity of warm air and cold air. Warm air is lighter than cold air and rises if cold air is available to replace it (see Figure 11).

a Operation — Satisfactory operation of a gravity-warm-air heating system depends on three factors. They are: (1) size of warm air and cold ducts, (2) heat loss of the building, (3) heat available from the furnace.

b Heat distribution — The most common source of trouble in these systems is insufficient pipe area usually in the return or cold air duct. The total cross-section area of the cold duct or ducts must be at least equal to the total cross-section area of all warm ducts.

c Pipeless furnaces — The pipeless hot-air furnace is the simplest type of hot-air furnace and is suitable for small homes where all rooms can be grouped about a single large register (see Figure 3). Other pipeless gravity furnaces are often installed at floor level. These are really oversized jacketed space heaters. The most common difficulty experienced with this type of furnace is supplying a return air opening of sufficient size on the floor.

2 Forced-Warm-Air Heating Systems —
The mechanical warm-air furnace is the most modern type of warm-air equipment (see Figure 12). It is the safest type because it operates at low temperatures. The principle of a forced-warm-air heating system is very similar to that of the gravity system, except that a fan or blower is added to increase air movement. Because of the assistance of the fan or blower, the pitch of the ducts or leaders can be disregarded and it is therefore practical to deliver heated air in the most convenient places.

a Operation — In a forced-air system, operation of the fan or blower must be controlled by air temperature in a bonnet or by a blower control furnacestat. The blower control starts the fan or blower when the temperature reaches a certain point and turns the fan or blower off when the temperature drops to a predetermined point.

b Heat distribution — Dampers in the various warm-air ducts control distribution

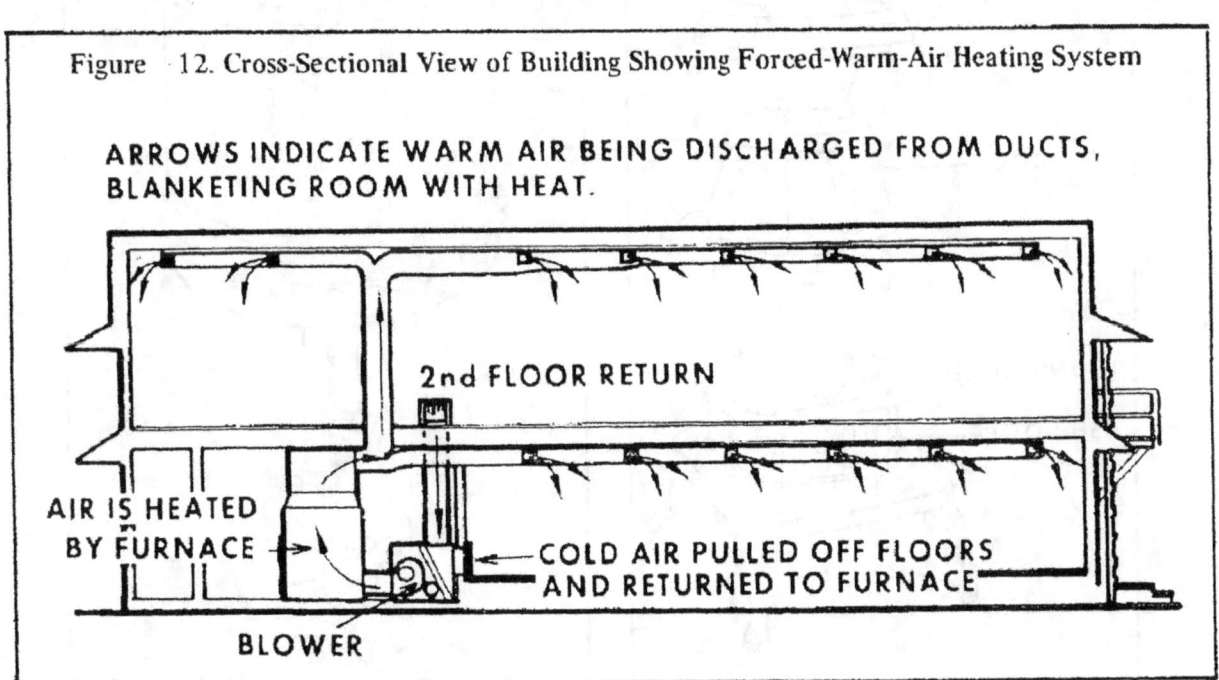

Figure 12. Cross-Sectional View of Building Showing Forced-Warm-Air Heating System

of warm air either at the branch takeoff or at the warm-air outlet.

Humidifiers are often mounted in the supply bonnet in order to regulate the humidity within the residence.

D Space Heaters — Space unit heaters are the least desirable from the viewpoint of fire safety and housing inspection. All space unit heaters must be vented to the flue.

1 Coal-Fired Space Heaters (Cannon stove) — This is illustrated in Figure 13 and is made entirely of cast iron. In operation, coal on the grates receives primary air for combustion through the grates from the ash-door draft intake. Combustible gases driven from the coal by heat burn in the barrel of the stove, where they received additional or secondary air through the feed door. Side and top of the stove absorb the heat of combustion and radiate it to the surrounding space.

2 Oil-Fired Space Heaters — Oil-fired space heaters have atmospheric vaporizing-type burners. The burners require a light grade of fuel oil that vaporizes easily and is comparatively low in temperature. In addition, the oil must be such that it leaves only a small amount of carbon residue and ash within the heater. Oil-fired space heaters are basically of two types:

a Perforated-sleeve burner — The perforated-sleeve burner (see Figure 14) consists essentially of a metal base formed of two or more angular fuel-vaporizing bowl burners (see Figure 15) and is widely used in space heaters and some water heaters.

The burner consists essentially of a bowl, 8 to 13 inches in diameter, with perforations in the side that admit air for combustion. The upper part of the bowl has a flame ring or collar. When several space heaters are installed in a building, an oil supply from an

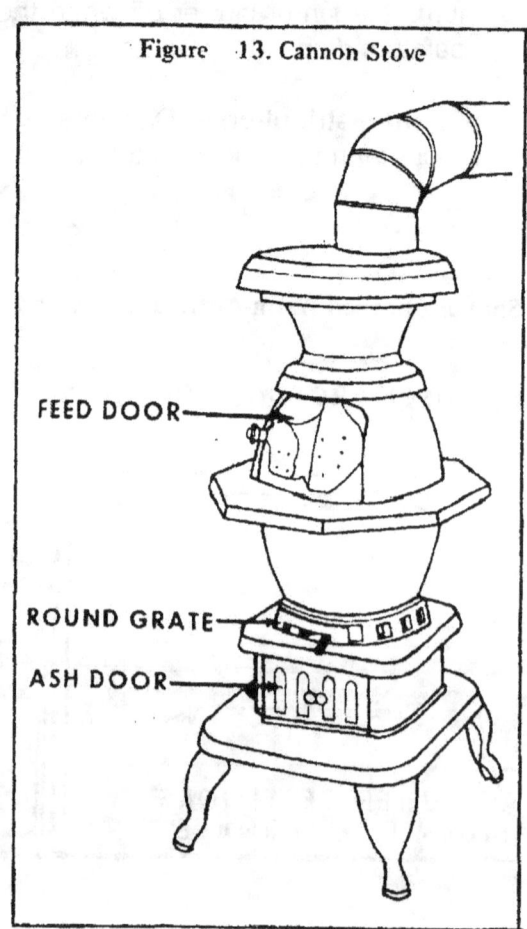

Figure 13. Cannon Stove

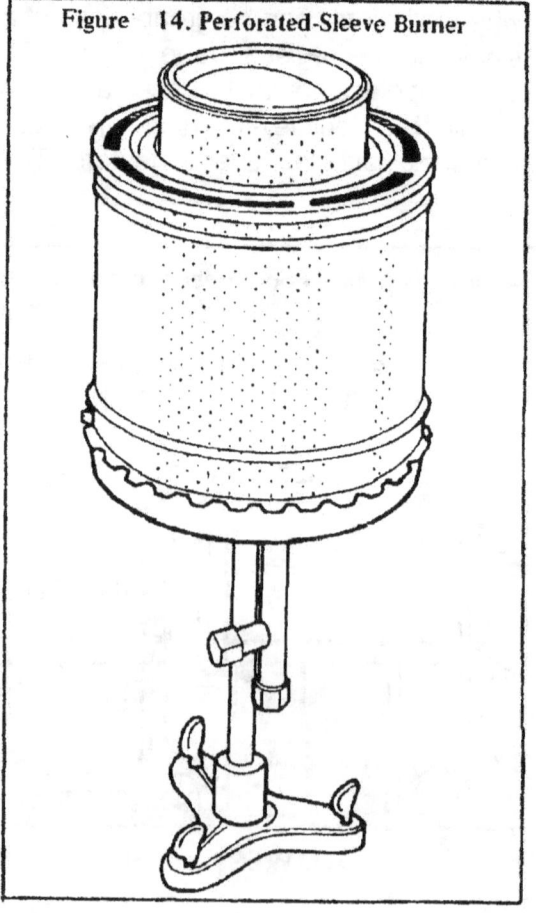

Figure 14. Perforated-Sleeve Burner

outside tank to all heaters is often desirable. Figure 16 shows the condition of a burner flame with different rates of fuel flow and indicates the ideal flame height.

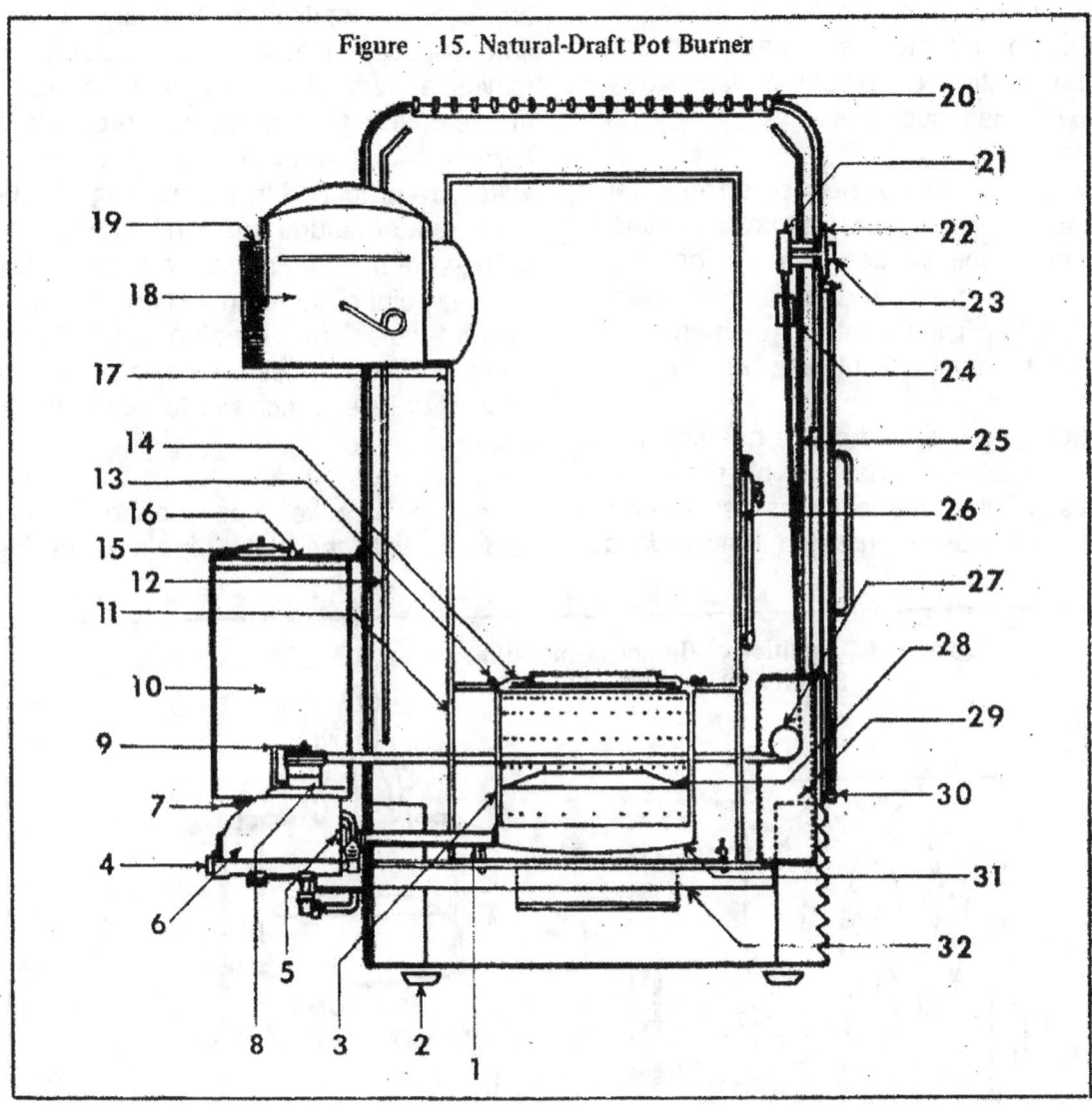

Figure 15. Natural-Draft Pot Burner

1   Burner-pot pipe.
2   Leg Leveler.
3   Pilot-ring clip.
4   Strainer unit.
5   Burner-pot drain plug.
6   Constant-level valve.
7   Tank valve
8   Control drum (to fit 6).
9   Control pulley bracket
10 Fuel tank.
11 Lower heat unit.
12 Heat shield (rear).
13 Burner-ring clamp.
14 Burner-top ring.
15 Fuel tank cap.
16 Tank fuel gauge.
17 Heat unit.
18 Cold draft regulator.
19 Flue connections, 6-inch diameter.
20 Top grille.
21 Dial control drum.
22 Escutcheon plate.
23 Dial control knob.
24 Pulley assembly (short).
25 Heat shield (front).
26 Heat-unit door.
27 Pulley assembly (long).
28 Pilot ring.
29 Humidifier.
30 Trim bar.
31 Burner pot.
32 Heat-unit support.

3 Gas-Fired Space Heaters—There are three types of gas-fired space heaters: natural, manufactured, and liquified petroleum gas. Space heaters using natural, manufactured, or liquified petroleum gases have a similar construction. All gas-fired space heaters must be vented to prevent a dangerous buildup of poisonous gases.

Each unit console consists of an enamel steel cabinet with top and bottom circulating grilles or openings, gas burners, heating element, gas pilot, and gas valve (see Figure 17). The heating element or combustion chamber is usually cast iron.

CAUTION: All gas-fired space heaters and their connections must be of the type approved by the American Gas Association (AGA). They must be installed in accordance with the recommendations of that organization or the local code.

a Venting — Use of proper venting materials and correct installation of venting for gas-fired space heaters is necessary to minimize harmful effects of condensation and to ensure that combustion products are carried off. (Approximately 12 gallons of water are produced in the burning of 1,000 cubic feet of natural gas. The inner surface of the vent must therefore be heated above the dewpoint of the combustion products to prevent water from forming in the flue.) A horizontal vent must be given an upward pitch of at least 1 inch per foot of horizontal distance.

When the smoke pipe extends through floors or walls the metal pipe must be insu-

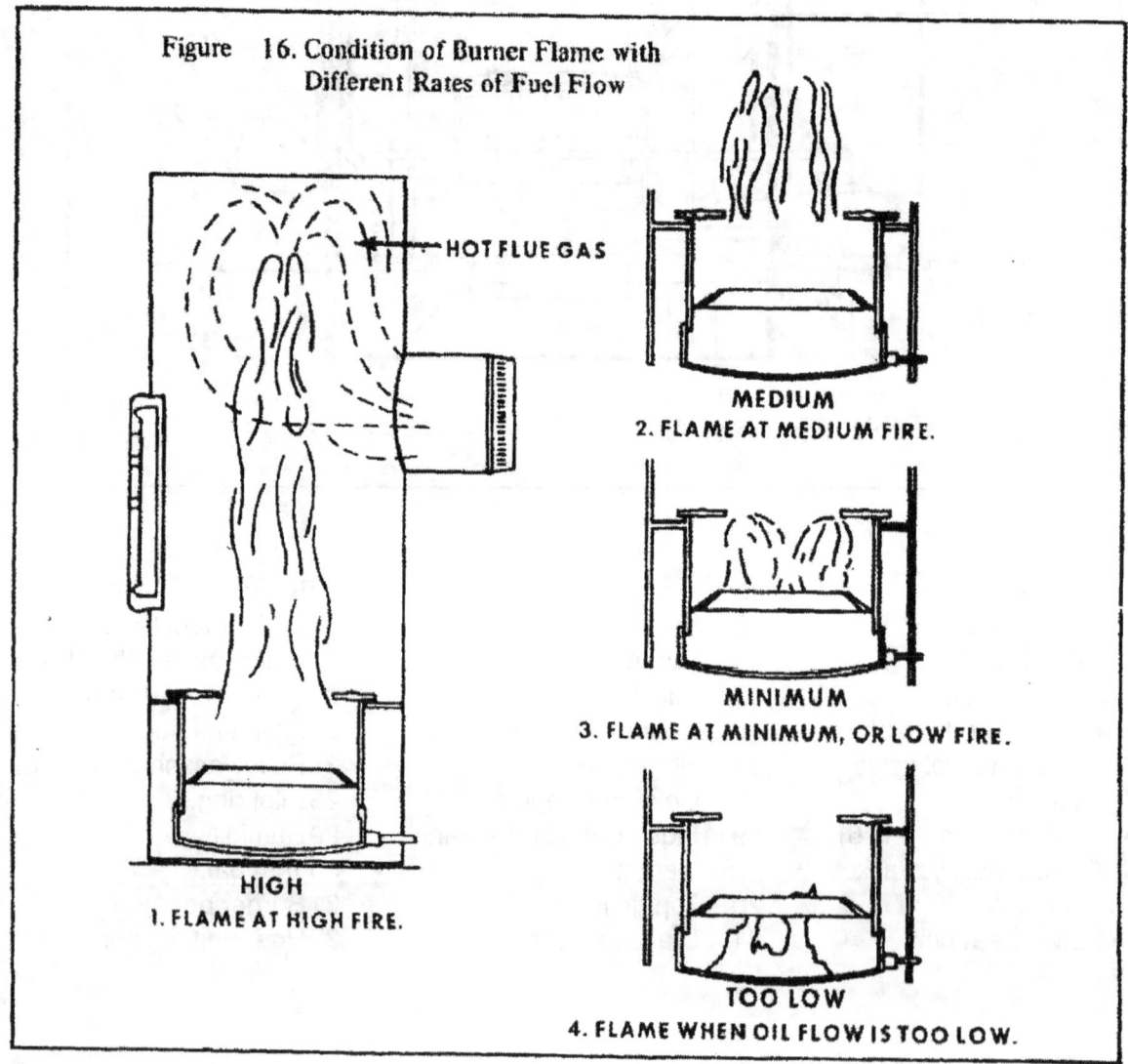

Figure 16. Condition of Burner Flame with Different Rates of Fuel Flow

1. FLAME AT HIGH FIRE.
2. FLAME AT MEDIUM FIRE.
3. FLAME AT MINIMUM, OR LOW FIRE.
4. FLAME WHEN OIL FLOW IS TOO LOW.

lated from the floor or wall system by an air space (see Figure 18). Avoid sharp bends. A 90° vent elbow has a resistance to flow equivalent to a straight section of pipe having a length of 10 times the elbow diameter. Be sure vent is of a rigid construction and resistant to corrosion by flue gas products. Several types of venting material are available such as B-vent and several other ceramic-type materials. A chimney lined with fire-brick type of terra cotta must be relined with an acceptable vent material if it is to be used for venting gas-fired appliances.

Use the same size vent pipe throughout its length. Never make a vent smaller than heater outlet except when two or more vents converge from separate heaters. To determine the size of vents beyond the point of convergence, add one-half the area of each vent to the area of the largest heater's vent.

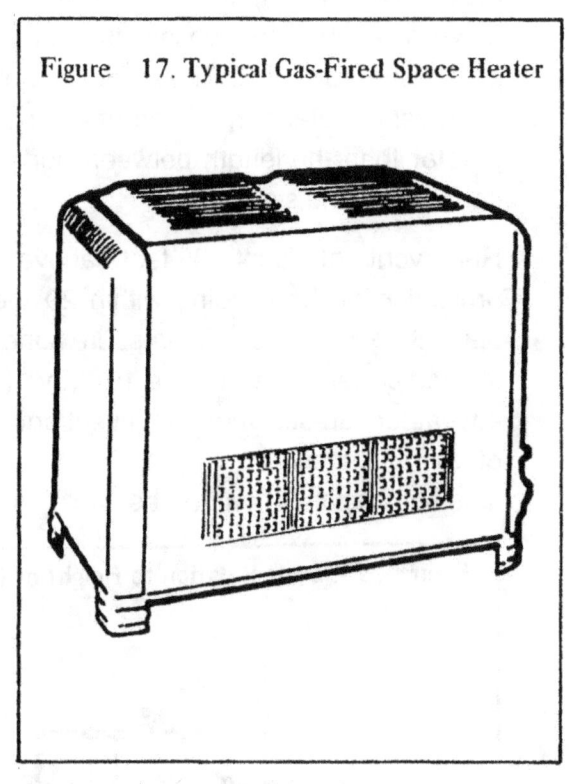

Figure 17. Typical Gas-Fired Space Heater

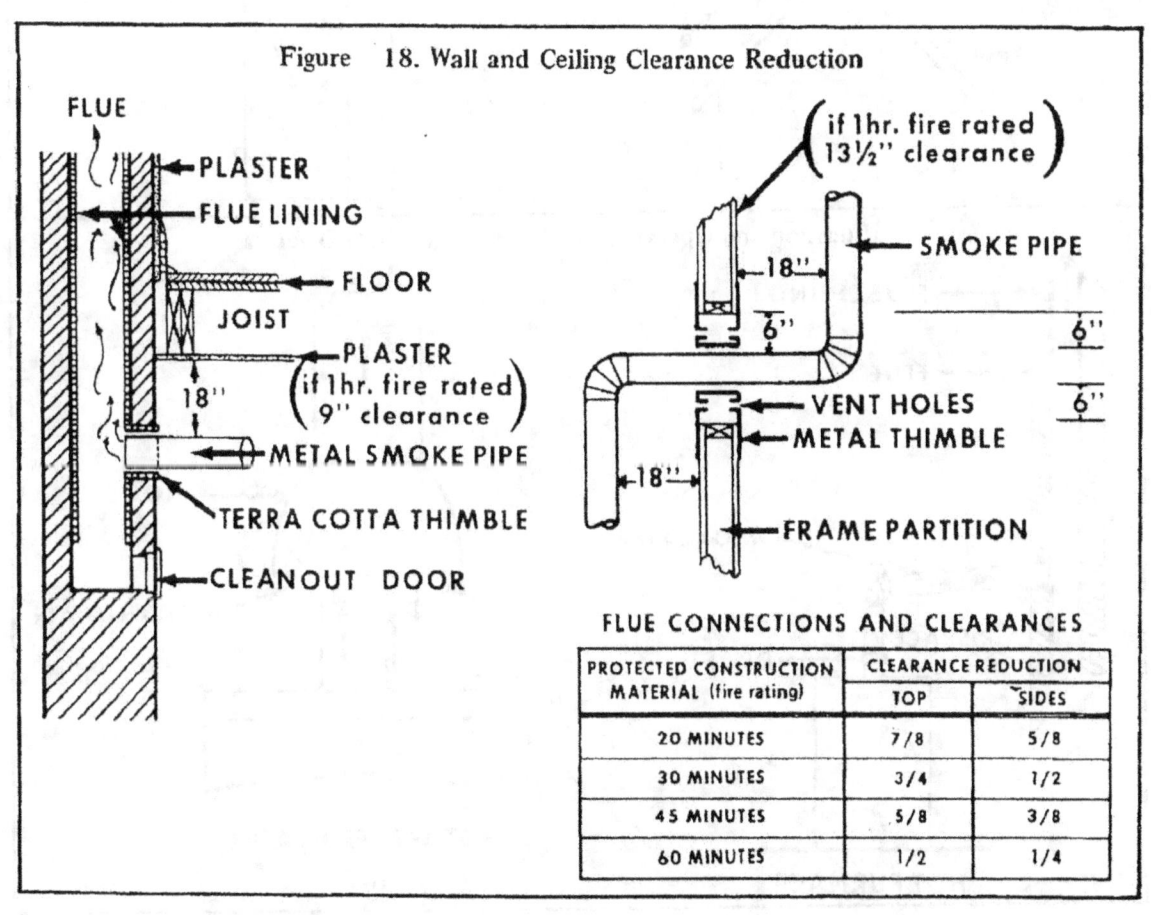

Figure 18. Wall and Ceiling Clearance Reduction

FLUE CONNECTIONS AND CLEARANCES

PROTECTED CONSTRUCTION MATERIAL (fire rating)	CLEARANCE REDUCTION	
	TOP	SIDES
20 MINUTES	7/8	5/8
30 MINUTES	3/4	1/2
45 MINUTES	5/8	3/8
60 MINUTES	1/2	1/4

Install vents with male ends of inner liner down to ensure condensate is kept within pipes on a cold start. The vertical length of each vent or stack should be at least 2 feet greater than the length between horizontal connection and stack.

Run vent at least 3 feet above any projection of the building within 20 feet to place it above a possible pressure zone due to wind currents (see Figure 19). End it with a weather cap designed to prevent entrance of rain and snow.

Gas-fired space heaters as well as gas furnaces and hot water heaters must be equipped with a backdraft diverter (see Figure ,20) designed to protect heaters against downdrafts and excessive updrafts. Use only draft diverters of the type approved by the AGA.

The combustion chamber or firebox must be insulated from the floor, usually with an airspace of 15 to 18 inches, or the firebox is sometimes insulated within the unit and thus allows for lesser clearance for combustibles.

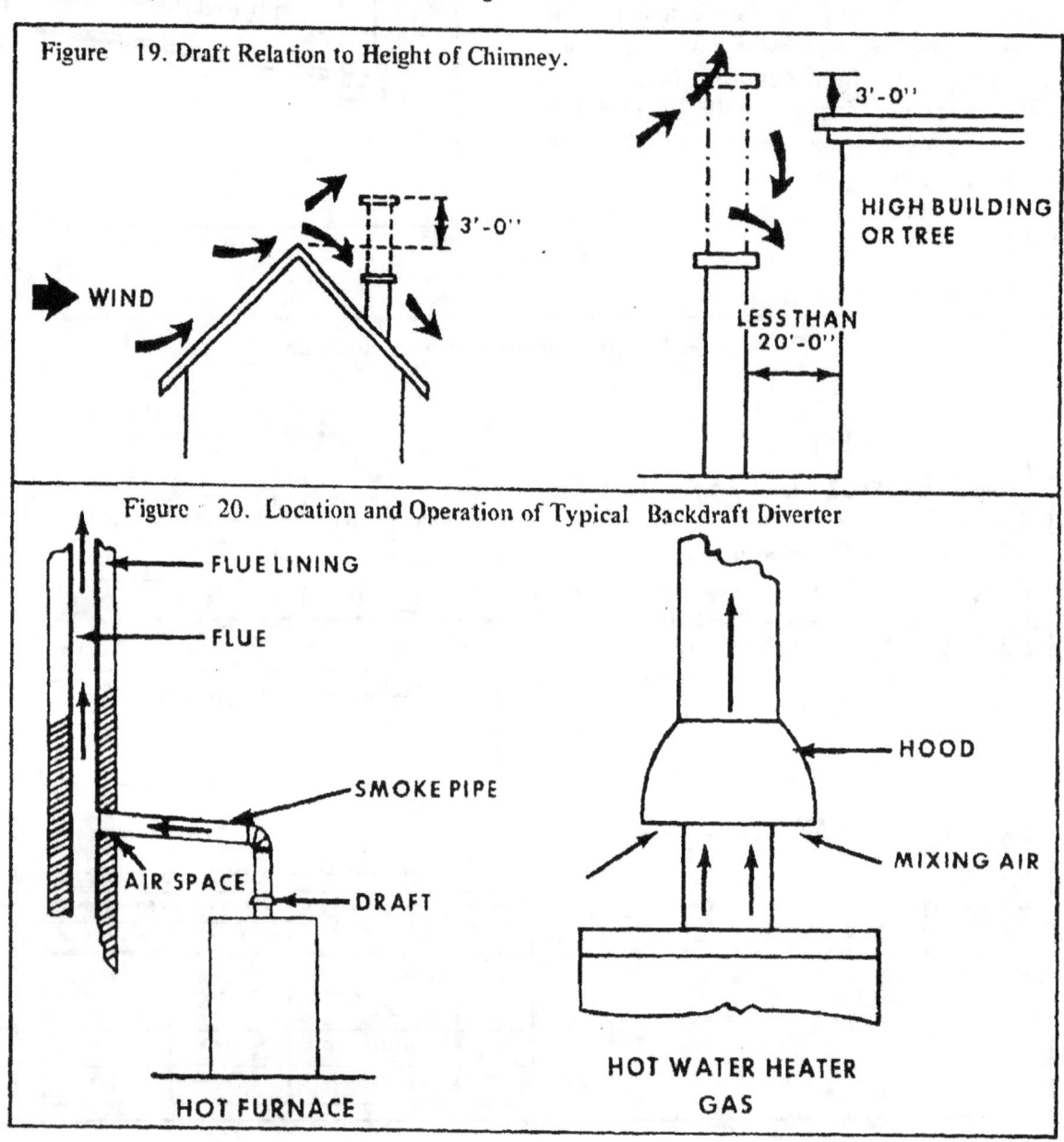

Figure 19. Draft Relation to Height of Chimney.

Figure 20. Location and Operation of Typical Backdraft Diverter

Where coal space heaters are located, a floor protection should be provided. This would be a metal-covered asbestos board or a similar durable insulation material. One reason for the floor protection would be to allow cooling off of hot coals and ashes if they drop out while ashes are being removed from the ash chamber. Walls and ceilings of a non-combustible construction exposed to furnace radiation should be installed, and the following clearances are recommended: Space heaters — A top or ceiling clearance of 36 inches, a wall clearance of 18 inches, and a smoke pipe clearance of 18 inches, (see Figure 18).

VIII. Domestic Hot Water Jack Stoves (Coal Stoves)

Domestic hot water jack stoves (coal stoves) equipped with water jackets to supply hot water for domestic use are to be treated as coal-fired furnaces or boilers previously discussed. Note that flue connections should not exceed two to the same flue unless the draft and size are sufficient to accommodate both exhausting requirements. One flue with one smoke pipe is the rule; however, housing inspectors may find a jack stove and main furnace connected to the same flue. Where these conditions are encountered and no complaint about malfunctioning of this system is found, it can be assumed that the system is operating satisfactorily. Where more than two units, other than gas, are attached to a single flue, the building agency should be notified, since this can be considered an improper installation. Gas, oil, and electric hot water heating units for domestic hot water should be treated the same as previously discussed for central heating units.

IX. Hazardous Installations

A **Generalities** — The housing inspector should be on the alert for unvented open burning flame heaters, such as manually operated gas logs. Coil-type wall-mounted hot-water heaters that do not have safety relief valves are not permitted. Kerosene (portable) units for cooking or heating should be prohibited. Generally, open-flame portable units are not allowed under fire safety regulations.

In oil heating units, other than integral tank units, the oil filling and vent must be located on the exterior of the building. Filling of oil within buildings is prohibited.

Electric wiring to heating units must be installed as indicated in the electrical section. Cutoff switches should be close to the entry but outside of the boiler room. The inspector should be able to appraise the heating installation and determine its adequacy. Any installation that indicates haphazard location, workmanship, or operation, whether it be building, zoning, plumbing, electrical, or housing, will dictate further inspection.

B **Chimneys (see Figure 21 and 22)** - Chimneys, as all inspectors know, are an integral part of the building. The chimney is a point of building safety and should be understood by the housing inspector. The chimney, if of masonry, must be tight and sound; flues should be terra cotta lined, and where no linings are installed, the brick should be tight to permit proper draft and elimination of combustion gases.

Chimneys that act as flues for gas-fired equipment must be lined with either B-vent or terra cotta.

To the inspector, on exterior inspection, "banana peel" on the portion of the chimney above the roof will indicate trouble and a need for rebuilding. Exterior deterioration of the chimney will, if let go too long, gradually permit erosion from within the flues and eventually block the flue opening.

Rusted flashing at the roof level will also contribute to the chimney's deterioration. Effervescence on the inside wall of the chimney below the roof and on the outside of the chimney, if exposed, will show salt accumulations — a tell-tale sign of water penetration and flue gas escape and a sign of chimney deterioration. In the spring and fall, during rain seasons, if terra cotta chimneys leak, the joint will be indicated by dark areas permitting actual counting of the number of flues inside the masonry chimney. When this condition occurs, it usually requires 2 or 3 months to dry out. Upon drying out, the mortar joints are discolored (brown), and so after a few years of this type of deterioration the joints can be distinguished wet or dry. The above-listed conditions usually develop during coal operation and become more pronounced usually 2 to 5 years after conversion to oil or gas.

An unlined chimney can be checked for deterioration below the roof line by checking the residue deposited at the base of the chimney, usually accessible through a cleanout (door or plug) or breaching. Red granular or fine powder showing through coal soot or oil soot will generally indicate, if in quantity (a handful), that deterioration is excessive and repairs are needed.

Gas units attached to unlined chimneys will be devoid of soot, but will usually show similar tell-tale brick powder and deterioration as previously mentioned. Manufactured gas has a greater tendency to dehydrate and decompose brick in chimney flues than natural gas. For gas installations in older homes, utility companies usually specify chimney requirements before installation, and so older chimneys may require the installation of terra cotta liners, lead-lined copper liners, or transite pipe. Oil burner operation using a low air ratio and high oil consumption is usually indicated by black carbon deposits around the top of the chimney. Prolonged operation in this burner setting results in long carbon water deposits down the chimney for 4 to 6 feet or more and should indicate to the inspector a possibility of poor burner maintenance. This will accent his need to be more thorough on the ensuing inspection. This type of condition can result from other related causes, such as improper chimney height or exterior obstructions such as trees or buildings that will cause downdrafts or insufficient draft or contribute to a faulty heating operation.

Rust spots and soot-mold usually occur on galvanized smoke pipe deterioration.

C Fireplace — Careful attention should be given to the construction of the fireplace. Improperly built fireplaces are a serious safety and fire hazard (see Figure 22). The most common causes of fireplace fires are thin walls, combustible materials such as studding or trim against sides and back of the fireplace, wood mantels, and unsafe hearths.

Fireplace walls should be not less than 8 inches thick, and if built of stone or hollow masonry units, not less than 12 inches thick. The faces of all walls exposed to fire should be lined with firebrick or other suitable fire-resistive material. When the lining consists of 4 inches of firebrick, such lining thickness may be included in the required minimum thickness of the wall.

The fireplace hearth should be constructed of brick, stone, tile, or similar incombustible material and should be supported on a fireproof slab or on a brick arch. The hearth should extend at least 20 inches beyond the chimney breast and not less than 12 inches beyond each side of the fireplace opening

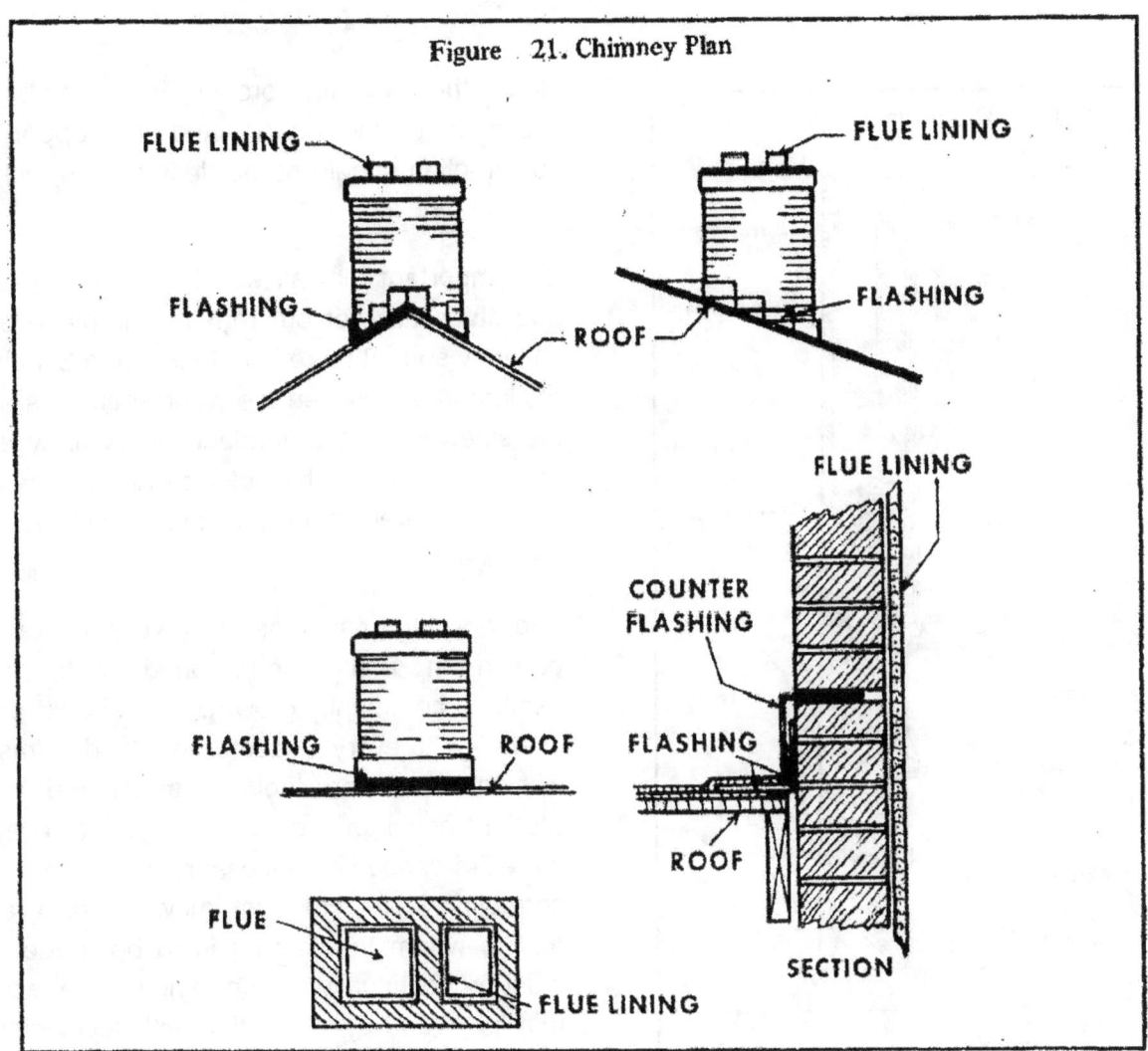

Figure 21. Chimney Plan

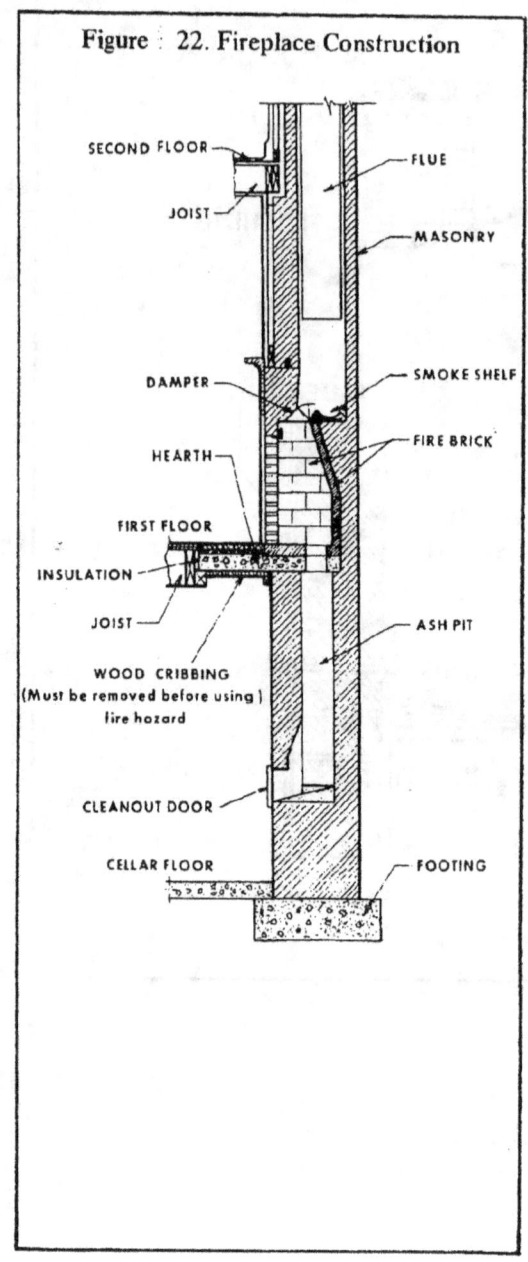

Figure 22. Fireplace Construction

along the chimney breast. The combined thickness of the hearth and its supporting construction should be not less than 6 inches at any point.

It is important that all wooden beams, joists, and studs are set off from the fireplace and chimney so that there is not less than 2 inches of clearance between the wood members and the sidewalls of the fireplace or chimney and not less than 4 inches of clearance between wood members and the back wall of the fireplace.

The housing inspector is a very important person in maintaining sound, safe, and healthful community growth. This should be a challenge to every inspector to provide himself with the necessary tools for better and more efficient housing inspection. He must develop the extra senses so necessary in spotting and correcting faults. He must know when to refer and to whom the referral is to be made; he must be continually seeking knowledge, which may be found by consulting with technicians, tradesmen, and professionals. No finer satisfaction can be realized than to know and feel that the security, safety, and comfort of each and every family within your community has a better and more healthful life because of that extra bit of knowledge you have imparted. "An inspector who stops learning today is uneducated tomorrow."

BASIC FUNDAMENTALS OF BOILERS

TABLE OF CONTENTS

		Page
I.	NATURE	1
II.	CLASSIFICATION	2
	A. Location of Fire and Water Spaces	2
	B. Size of Tubes	2
	C. Type of Circulation	2
	D. Type of Superheat	3
III.	TERMINOLOGY	3
	A. Fire Room and Boiler Room	4
	B. Boiler Emergency Station	4
	C. Boiler Full-Power Capacity	4
	D. Boiler Overload Capacity	4
	E. Superheater Outlet Pressure	4
	F. Steam Drum Pressure	4
	G. Design Pressure	4
	H. Operating Pressure	4
	I. Boiler Efficiency	4
	J. Fire Room Efficiency	4
	K. Total Heating Surface	5
	L. Generating Surface	5
	M. Superheater Surface	5
	N. Economizer Surface	5
	O. Steaming Hours	5

BASIC FUNDAMENTALS OF BOILERS

I. NATURE

The boiler is the source or high-temperature region of the thermos-dynamic cycle. The steam that is generated in the boiler is led to the turbines, where its thermal energy is converted into mechanical energy (work) which drives the unit and provides power for vital services.

In essence, a boiler is merely a container in which water can be boiled and steam generated. A tea kettle on a stove is basically a boiler, although a rather inefficient one. Note that the steam is generated in one vessel and superheated in another, since it is impossible to raise the temperature of the steam above the temperature of the boiling water as long as the two are in contact with each other.

In designing a boiler which must produce a large amount of steam, it is obviously necessary to find some means of providing a larger amount of heat-transfer surface than could be provided by a vessel shaped like a tea kettle. In most modern boilers, the steam generating surface consists of hundreds and hundreds of tubes, which provide a maximum amount of heat-transfer surface in a relatively small space. As a rule, the tubes communicate with a steam drum at the top of a boiler and with water drums and headers at the bottom of the boiler. The tubes and part of the drums are enclosed in an insulated capsule which has space inside it for the furnace. A boiler appears to be a fairly complicated piece of equipment when it is considered with all its fittings, piping, and accessories; it may be helpful, therefore, to remember that the basic components of a saturated-steam boiler are merely the tubes, the drums, and headers, and the furnace.

Practically all boilers used in propulsion are designed to produce both saturated steam and superheated steam. To our basic boiler, therefore, we must now add another component: the superheater. The superheater on most boilers consist of headers, usually located at the back of the boiler, and a number of superheater tubes which communicate with the headers. Saturated steam from the steam drum is led through the superheater; since the steam is now no longer in contact with the water from which it was generated, the steam becomes superheated as additional heat is supplied. In some boilers, there is a separate superheater furnace; in others, the superheater tubes project into the same furnace that is used for the generation of saturated steam.

Some question may arise concerning the need for both saturated steam and superheated steam. Saturated steam is used for operating most steam-driven auxiliary machinery; reciprocating machinery, in particular, requires saturated steam for the lubrication of the moving parts of the steam end. Superheated steam is used almost exclusively for the propulsion turbines. There is more available energy in superheated steam than in saturated steam at the same pressure; and the use of higher temperatures vastly increases the efficiency of the propulsion cycle since, as we have seen, the efficiency of a heat engine is dependent upon the absolute temperature at the source (boiler) and the absolute temperature at the receiver (condenser). In some instances, the gain in efficiency resulting from the use of superheated steam may be as much as 15 percent for 200 degrees of superheat. This increase in efficiency is particularly important because it allows substantial savings in fuel consumption and in space and weight requirements. A further advantage in using superheated steam for propulsion machinery is that it causes relatively little erosion since it is free of moisture

II. CLASSIFICATION

Boilers may be classified in a number of different ways, according to various design features. Most commonly, they are classified and described in terms of (1) the relative location of the fire and water spaces, (2) the size of the tubes, (3) the type of circulation, and (4) the type of superheat. Some knowledge of these methods of classification will be useful in understanding the design and construction of modern boilers.

    A. Location of Fire and Water Spaces

First of all, boilers are classified according to the relative location of their fire and water spaces. By this classification, all boilers may be divided into two groups: *fire-tube boilers* and *water-tube boilers*. In *fire-tube boilers*, the gases of combustion flow through the tubes and thereby heat the surrounding water. In *water-tube boilers*, the water flows through the tubes and is heated by the gases of combustion that fill the furnace.

    B. Size of Tubes

Water-tube boilers are further classified according to the size of the tubes. Boilers having tubes 2 inches or more in diameter are called *large-tube boilers*. Boilers having tubes less than 2 inches in diameter are called *small-tube* or *express-type boilers*.

    C. Type of Circulation

Water-tube boilers are also classified as *natural circulation boilers* or as *force circulation boilers*, depending upon the way in which the water circulates within the boiler.

Natural circulation boilers are those in which the circulation of water depends upon the difference in density between an ascending mixture of hot water and steam and a descending body of relatively cool and steam-free water. Natural circulation may be of two types, free or accelerated.

In this type of boiler, the generating tubes are installed at a slight angle of inclination which allows the lighter hot water and steam to rise while the cooler (and heavier) water descends.

Installing the generating tubes at a greater angle of inclination increases the rate of water circulation. Hence, boilers in which the tubes slope more steeply are said to have accelerated natural circulation.

Most modern boilers are designed for accelerated natural circulation. In such boilers, large tubes (3 or more inches in diameter) are installed between the steam drum and the water drums. These tubes, called *downcomers*, are located outside the furnace and away from the heat of combustion, thereby serving as pathways for the downward flow of relatively cool water. When a sufficient number of downcomers are installed, all small tubes can be generating tubes, carrying steam and water upward; and all downward flow can be carried by the downcomer. The size and number of downcomers installed varies from one type of boiler to another.

Forced circulation boilers are, as their name implies, quite different in design from the boilers that utilize natural circulation. Instead of depending upon differences in density between the hotter and the cooler water, forced circulation boilers use pumps to force the water through the various boiler circuits. Forced circulation boilers are relatively new, but they have some very definite advantages which will probably lead to their increased use in the future.

   D. Type of Superheat

Practically all boilers are equipped with superheaters. With respect to the superheater installation, boilers are classified as having either controlled superheat or uncontrolled superheat. In a boiler with *controlled superheat*, the degree of superheat can be changed by regulating the amount of heat supplied to the superheater tube bank, without substantially changing the amount of heat supplied to the generating tubes. This control of superheat is possible because the boiler has two furnaces, one for the saturated side and one for the superheat side. A boiler with *uncontrolled superheat*, on the other hand, has only one furnace; and since the same furnace must be used for heating both the generating tubes and the superheater tubes, the degree of superheat cannot be controlled but varies within a small range as a function of design and firing rate.

Various terms are used to describe these two basic types of superheaters. Where the superheat is controlled, the superheater is often referred to as an *integral, separately fired superheat*, and the boiler as a whole is called a *superheat control boiler*. Where the superheat is not controlled, the superheater may be called an *integral, not separately fired superheater*, or it may be referred to as a *no control, or uncontrolled superheater*, and the boiler as a whole is called a *no control or uncontrolled superheat boiler*. The term *integral* is used to indicate that the superheater is installed as a part of the boiler unit. Practically all superheaters on modern boilers are integral with the boilers.

On both controlled and uncontrolled superheat boilers, the superheater tubes are protected from radiant heat by generation tubes that are called *water screen tubes*. The water screen tubes absorb the intense radiant heat of the furnace, and the superheater tubes are heated by convection currents rather than by direct radiation. Hence, the superheaters are sometimes called *convection-type superheaters*.

Some older types of superheat control boilers had *radiant-type superheaters*—that is, the superheater tubes were not screened by water tubes but were exposed directly to the radiant heat of the furnace. However, this type of superheater is relatively uncommon at the present time and will, therefore, not be further discussed.

III. TERMINOLOGY

In order to ensure uniform use of terms, there has been established a number of standard terms and definitions pertaining to boilers. Some of the more important of these definitions are given below.

A. Fire Room and Boiler Room: A compartment which contains boilers and the station for operating them is called a *fire room*. A compartment which contains boilers which does not contain the station for operating them is called a *boiler room*.

B. Boiler Emergency Station: This term is used to designate a station which is so located that, in the event of trouble, one may proceed with minimum delay to any fire room, boiler operating station, or boiler room.

C. Boiler Full-Power Capacity: The total quantity of steam required to develop contract shaft horsepower of the vessel, divided by the number of boilers installed, gives boiler full-power capacity. The quantity of steam is given in pounds of water evaporated per hour. Full-power capacity is indicated in the manufacturer's technical manual for each boiler.

D. Boiler Overload Capacity: Boiler overload capacity is specified in the design of the boiler. It is given in terms of steaming rate or firing rate, depending upon the individual installation. Boiler overload capacity is usually 120 percent of boiler full-power capacity.

E. Superheater Outlet Pressure: This is the actual steam pressure at the superheater outlet.

F. Steam Drum Pressure: This is the pressure in the steam drum. Steam drum pressure is specified in the design of a boiler and is given in the manufacturer's technical manual for each boiler. Steam drum pressure is the pressure which must be carried in the boiler steam drum in order to obtain the required pressure at the turbine throttles, when steaming at full-power capacity. Ordinarily, the designed steam drum pressure is carried for all steaming conditions.

G. Design Pressure: Design pressure is the pressure specified by the boiler manufacturer as a criterion for boiler design. It is usually 103 percent of steam drum pressure.

H. Operating Pressure: Operating pressure is the pressure at the final outlet from a boiler, after steam has passed through all baffles, the dry pipe, the superheater, etc., when the boiler is steaming at full-power capacity. Operating pressure is specified in the design of a boiler and is given in the manufacturer's technical manual. Operating pressure is the same as superheater outlet pressure when the boiler is steaming at full-power capacity; when the boiler is steaming at less than full-power capacity, however, the actual pressure at the superheater outlet will vary from the specified operating pressure provided a constant drum pressure is maintained.

I. Boiler Efficiency: The efficiency of a boiler is the British thermal units per pound of fuel absorbed by the water and steam divided by the British thermal units per pound of fuel fired. In other words, boiler efficiency is output divided by input, or Btu utilized divided by Btu available. Boiler efficiency is expressed as a percentage.

J. Fire Room Efficiency: The boiler efficiency corrected for blower and pump steam consumption is known as fire room efficiency. (This is not the same as boiler plant efficiency or propulsion plant efficiency.)

K. Total Heating Surface: The total heating surface of any steam generating unit consists of that portion of the heat transfer apparatus which is exposed on one side to the gases of combustion and on the other side to the water or steam being heated. Thus, the total heating surface equals the sum of the generating surface, the superheater surface, and the economizer surface. All heating surfaces are measured on the combustion-gas side.

L. Generating Surface: The generating surface is that portion of the total heating surface in which the fluid being heated forms part of the circulating system. The generating surface includes the boiler tube banks, water walls, water screens, and water floors (where installed and not covered by refractory material.)

M. Superheater Surface: The superheater surface is that portion of the total heating surface where the steam is heated after leaving the boiler steam drum.

N. Economizer Surface: The economizer surface is that portion of the total heating surface where the feed water is heated before entering the generating system.

O. Steaming Hours: The term steaming hours includes the time during which the boiler has fires lighted for raising steam and the time during which it is generating steam. Time during which fires are not lighted is not included in steaming hours.